I0411783

I'll love you, dear, I'll love you till China and Africa meet and the river jumps over the mountain and the salmon sing in the street.

W. H. Auden

I will not leave South Africa, nor will I surrender. Only through hardship, sacrifice and militant action can freedom be won. The struggle is my life. I will continue fighting for freedom until the end of my days.

Nelson Mandela

One individual can begin a movement that turns the tide of history. Martin Luther King in the civil rights movement, Mohandas Ganhi in India, Nelson Mandela in South Africa are examples of people standing up with courage and non-violence to bring about needed changes.

Jack Canfield

You can't hate the roots of a tree and not hate the tree. You can't hate Africa and not hate yourself.

Malcolm X

When the missionaries came to Africa they had the Bible and we had the land. They said 'Let us pray.' We closed our eyes. When we opened them we had the Bible and they had the land.

Desmond Tutu

The drums of Africa still beat in my heart. They will not let me rest while there is a single Negro boy or girl without a chance to prove his worth.

Mary McLeod Bethune

The last four or five hundred years of European contact with Africa produced a body of literature that presented Africa in a very bad light and Africans in very lurid terms. The reason for this had to do with the need to justify the slave trade and slavery.

Chinua Achebe

All the armies of Europe, Asia and Africa combined, with all the treasure of the earth (our own excepted) in their military chest; with a Buonaparte for a commander, could not by force, take a drink from the Ohio, or make a track on the Blue Ridge, in a trial of a thousand years.

Abraham Lincoln

In my country of South Africa, we struggled for years against the evil system of apartheid that divided human beings, children of the same God, by racial classification and then denied many of them fundamental human rights.

Desmond Tutu

It is easy to romanticize poverty, to see poor people as inherently lacking agency and will. It is easy to strip them of human dignity, to reduce them to objects of pity. This has never been clearer than in the view of Africa from the American media, in which we are shown poverty and conflicts without any context.

Chimamanda Ngozi Adichie

I dream of the realization of the unity of Africa, whereby its leaders combine in their efforts to solve the problems of this continent. I dream of our vast deserts, of our forests, of all our great wildernesses.

Nelson Mandela

I have no desire to take all black people back to Africa; there are blacks who are no good here and will likewise be no good there.

Marcus Garvey

The future belongs to us, because we have taken charge of it. We have the commitment, we have the resourcefulness, and we have the strength of our people to share the dream across Africa of clean water for all.

Ellen Johnson Sirleaf

Our success educationally, industrially and politically is based upon the protection of a nation founded by ourselves. And the nation can be nowhere else but in Africa.

Marcus Garvey

People think that you have to do something huge, like go to Africa and build a school, but you can make a small change in a day. If you change Wednesday, then you change Thursday. Pretty soon it's a week, then a month, then a year. It's bite-size, as opposed to feeling like you have to turn your life inside out to make changes.

Hoda Kotb

If I were not African, I wonder whether it would be clear to me that Africa is a place where the people do not need limp gifts of fish but sturdy fishing rods and fair access to the pond. I wonder whether I would realize that while African nations have a failure of leadership, they also have dynamic people with agency and voices.

Chimamanda Ngozi Adichie

They talk about the failure of socialism but where is the success of capitalism in Africa, Asia and Latin America?

Fidel Castro

In South Africa, we could not have achieved our freedom and just peace without the help of people around the world, who through the use of non-violent means, such as boycotts and divestment, encouraged their governments and other corporate actors to reverse decades-long support for the Apartheid regime.

Desmond Tutu

Clean water and access to food are some of the simplest things that we can take for granted each and every day. In places like Africa, these can be some of the hardest resources to attain if you live in a rural area.

Marcus Samuelsson

I dream of an Africa which is in peace with itself.

Nelson Mandela

Reminds me of my safari in Africa. Somebody forgot the corkscrew and for several days we had to live on nothing but food and water.

W. C. Fields

No matter what vision one has of South Africa, the first thing that must be done is to destroy racism.

Joe Slovo

The white man is not indigenous to Africa. Africa is for Africans. Zimbabwe is for Zimbabweans.

Robert Mugabe

All of my life had been spent in the shadow of apartheid. And when South Africa went through its extraordinary change in 1994, it was like having spent a lifetime in a boxing ring with an opponent and suddenly finding yourself in that boxing ring with nobody else and realising you've to take the gloves off and get out, and reinvent yourself.

Athol Fugard

Inspiring scenes of people taking the future of their countries into their own hands will ignite greater demands for good governance and political reform elsewhere in the world, including in Asia and in Africa.

William Hague

Decolonization actually boosted slavery. As foreign powers withdrew from the colonies, people were enslaved by their own countrymen. And we see it in Africa, we see it in Asia.

Loretta Napoleoni

We filmed 'Labyrinth' in South Africa for two and a half months and it was just the most unbelievable experience. Lots of sword fighting, mud in hair and lots of weeping! It's very different from 'Downton' because I was going to work and having mud put in my hair - it's the other extreme of the look!

Jessica Brown Findlay

I like to go to Africa purely with something to do. I'm not very comfortable getting into an armor-plated Land Rover and going to see things, with my hand gel, you know, it's not me at all. So I like to hang out and you know, really get to know people and try and do something that resonates with them.

Damon Albarn

No one could seriously dispute that almost all of sub-Saharan Africa, all of North Africa except Morocco, all of the Middle East except Israel and Jordan and most of the oil-rich states, and the entire former British Indian Empire were better governed by Europeans.

Conrad Black

I first heard African drum rhythms and chants at the movies. Then, when I had the opportunity to go to Africa and visit the villages, I heard the real, raw, true rhythms and realised the origins of the old Negro spirituals I grew up with in the South.

Isaac Hayes

I want us to be judged by the impact we have on the health of the people of Africa and the health of women. Improvements in the health of the people of Africa and the health of women are key indicators of the performance of WHO. This is a health organization for the whole world... But we must focus our attention on the people in greatest need.

Margaret Chan

Basketball Without Borders is a leadership camp that takes basketball to different places around the world, to Africa, Europe, America and Asia. It's a camp that brings players from different parts of the continent to one city that's been assigned as the host city. We've been going to a different city every year.

Dikembe Mutombo

I went to South Africa on safari and came eye to eye with a beautiful leopard. We were so close; I was staring at him for a long time and I felt a recognition with my own nature.

Bai Ling

In this era of the global village, the tide of democracy is running. And it will not cease, not in China, not in South Africa, not in any corner of this earth, where the simple idea of democracy and freedom has taken root.

Paul Tsongas

Personally, I believe in self-determination, but in the context of one South Africa - so that my self-determination is based in this region, and with my people.

Mangosuthu Buthelezi

There is but little room for doubt that Egypt led the way in the creation of the earliest known group of civilizations which arose on both sides of the land bridge between Africa and Eurasia in the fourth millennium B.C.

James Henry Breasted

Personally, I regard myself as an intellectual 'rebel,' kicking against the 'old colonialism-imperialism paradigm' which has landed Africa in a conundrum.

George Ayittey

I am on my way to Ghana tomorrow morning and you just need to know that this Administration is very focused on doing all we can to promote economic development in this part of the world, in Africa, throughout Africa, North Africa and sub-Saharan Africa.

Donald Evans

The funny thing about war is that people feel you need to be morally outraged. I feel morally outraged about it, and I've been doing it for long enough to feel morally outraged, because I have been in massacre scenes in West Africa, and I've been doing this for a long time now.

Tim Hetherington

After I made it to the NBA, I said that I didn't want to be the last player from Africa. After my rookie year, I went to the league and talked about this, and they embraced my idea and started conducting basketball clinics in Africa, and that's when I knew I wouldn't be the last African.

Dikembe Mutombo

Coming from Morocco was just different, man. It's a third-world country, and you are trying to make it happen. That's all it is. I didn't have any problem hooking up with the black kids because I'm from North Africa. And as far as Latinos, we are all the same.

French Montana

My two must-haves are my cell phone and my MacBook Pro laptop, which allows me to update my Web site from wherever I am, whether I'm in Africa or in Sun Valley skiing.

Daryn Kagan

There are few people who define the word, 'rock star' better than U2's Bono. He's revered the world over not just for leading one of the biggest bands ever, but for his very public work on behalf of the underprivileged in Africa.

Daryn Kagan

I just came from South Africa, a place that had been in a perpetual uprising since 1653, so the uprising had become a way of life in our culture and we grew up with rallies and strikes and marches and boycotts.

Hugh Masekela

The government that came into power after the April 1994 elections was going to need a budget. It was drafted by our finance minister, Derek Keys, and he convinced them of the necessity to stay within the free-market principles that had been in force in South Africa for decades.

F. W. de Klerk

White sharks and tuna travel for thousands of miles before returning to the same hot spot just as salmon do when they return to the same stream. These journeys are the marine equivalent of wildebeest migrations that take place on the Serengeti plain in Africa.

Barbara Block

We cannot continually barricade ourselves under some falsified idea of race, because our idea of blackness and race is simply reactionary. Africans didn't walk around Africa being black and proud, they walked around proud.

Saul Williams

This is my first visit to Africa, a region where President Bush has voiced a deep passion for fostering and encouraging economic development, investment and trade.

Donald Evans

Of all the creatures in the world that really frighten me - the hyena in Africa, the great white shark - leopard seals are near the top of the list. They're killers. If my team spots one, they'll pull me out of the water.

Lewis Gordon Pugh

I lived in South Africa until I was 11 when we first immigrated. My mom had sent me back there when I was 14 for summer vacation. I wasn't doing very well in school, my grades were slipping. I called my mom one day and told her that I wasn't coming back. I ended up staying there until I was 17 before coming back to North America.

Kandyse McClure

Africa is going through its own historical process of state formation just as Europe and America did. It is just happening much later than other continents because of the interruption of Africa's own historical development by the colonization of Africa by Europe.

John Prendergast

South Africa is the only place in the Southern hemisphere where Halloween is really catching on. They have a lot of sporting events that have made it more popular there. They have motocross and rave celebrations, and they're embracing it as a youth culture thing.

Lisa Morton

I like the idea of readers feeling a familiarity, whether it's with Africa or childhood.

Binyavanga Wainaina

One of the challenges for sub-Saharan Africa is that markets are of modest size. This makes regional integration important.

Robert Zoellick

The future of Africa is in innovative engineering.

Erik Hersman

I grew up on a dairy farm in Southeastern Connecticut, and I went into the Peace Corps right after college. I went to Ghana. I fell in love with Africa and have basically been working in Africa ever since.

Bruce Wilkinson

I went to Africa without the perspective of a balance between teaching people the truth, which has been my calling, and helping people who have physical problems, like AIDS and orphans and hunger.

Bruce Wilkinson

In the following pages I have endeavoured to describe all that appeared to me most important and interesting among the events and the scenes that came under my notice during my sojourn in the interior of Africa.

John Hanning Speke

I'd the upbringing a nun would envy. Until I was fifteen I was more familiar with Africa than my own body.

Joe Orton

No one can compare us to the apartheid regime. It's not like in South Africa between the blacks and the whites who belong to the same nation, or in Berlin where you find parents living on the eastern side and their children in the western side.

Silvan Shalom

Taking the entire globe, if North America and Western Europe can be called the 'cities of the world', then Asia, Africa and Latin America constitute 'the rural areas of the world'.

Lin Biao

Growing up in this post-apartheid era, the first generation of teens in South Africa living in this new democracy, I often found myself feeling different. I was often the only person of color in an otherwise all-white school. And within the Indian community, because of my training with an English acting teacher, my accent was very different.

Adhir Kalyan

I got to Africa. I got the opportunity to go and learn, not about any animal, but chimpanzees. I was living in my dream world, the forest in Gombe National Park in Tanzania. It was Tanganyika when I began.

Jane Goodall

With the kinds of progress we're seeing in Africa, we have people who have a very high expectation, and often people think that, you know, things would happen overnight. But I want people to understand that sometimes it even gets worse before it gets better.

John Dramani Mahama

An insuperable obstacle to rapid transit in Africa is the want of carriers, and as speed was the main object of the Expedition under my command, my duty was to lessen this difficulty as much as possible.

Henry Morton Stanley

The fact is that ours is the first generation that can look disease and extreme poverty in the eye, look across the ocean to Africa, and say this, and mean it. We do not have to stand for this. A whole continent written off - we do not have to stand for this.

Bono

Jazz is known all over the world as an American musical art form and that's it. No America, no jazz. I've seen people try to connect it to other countries, for instance to Africa, but it doesn't have a damn thing to do with Africa.

Art Blakey

People say that slaves were taken from Africa. This is not true: People were taken from Africa, among them healers and priests, and were made into slaves.

Abdullah Ibrahim

I don't share the view that the ICC is anti-African. The ICC is not putting Africa on trial. The ICC is fighting impunity and individuals who are accused of crimes.

Kofi Annan

Do you think that the people of South Africa, or anywhere on the continent of Africa, or India, or Pakistan are longing to be kicked around all over again?

Arundhati Roy

Blacks in the Caribbean, Britain, Canada and sub-Saharan Africa as well as in the United States have low IQ scores relative to whites.

J. Philippe Rushton

I have been blessed in many ways, and one of those is to have been born in Africa, for me a great treasure house of stories. I have been researching it since my infancy; reading about it, talking to men and women who have spent their lives in this land, living it as I have and loving it as I do. I write almost entirely from my own experience.

Wilbur Smith

I envision someday a great, peaceful South Africa in which the world will take pride, a nation in which each of many

different groups will be making its own creative
contribution.

Alan Paton

When I was born, my dad and my mom gave me names,
but in Africa, when your child is born, especially close
family members can suggest names they want to add on.
Maybe your grandmom and your grandpop have something
to add to the name of the child.

Dikembe Mutombo

In Sub-Saharan Africa, where agriculture represents two-
thirds of all employment, governments are proving that
resource commitments yield success. In 2004, African
heads of state pledged 10 percent of their national budgets
to achieve 6 percent annual growth in agriculture. By 2008,
20 African countries had met or exceeded that 6 percent
target.

Sylvia Mathews Burwell

Obviously when it comes to the question of telling stories
about other people's lives in a situation as political as South
Africa, you get to be political.

Athol Fugard

As Ethiopia goes, so goes the whole Horn of Africa - a region where instability can have major security and humanitarian implications for the United States and Europe.

Eskinder Nega

I played an integral part in helpings formulating that new vision... that we must abandon apartheid and accept one united South Africa with equal rights for all, with all forms of discrimination to be scrapped from the statute book.

F. W. de Klerk

The only people who can fix Africa are talented young Africans. By unlocking and nurturing their creative potential, we can create a step change in Africa's future.

Neil Turok

Just as it is important in Latin America to discuss ideas that come from North America, I think it is interesting for North Americans to discuss ideas that come from Latin America or Africa and do not insert themselves into capitalist interests.

Paulo Freire

I think all of my writing life led up to the writing of 'The Train Driver' because it deals with my own inherited blindness and guilt and all of what being a white South African in South Africa during those apartheid years meant.

Athol Fugard

I think the aloe is one of South Africa's most powerful, beautiful and celebratory symbols. It survives out there in the wild when everything else is dried.

Athol Fugard

I'm from the '60s, but no one has ever accused me of being a hippie. I never had much interest in the Woodstock crowd, which partied to change the world, while real people were starving to death in Africa.

Lloyd Kaufman

I had intended to have gone into Africa incognito. But the fact that a white man, even an American, was about to enter Africa was soon known all over Zanzibar.

Henry Morton Stanley

We say that the ICC is targeting Africans, but all of the victims in our cases in Africa are African victims.

Fatou Bensouda

Clean water and power is our right as humans on this earth, and for too long, our governments in Africa have failed to provide these things.

William Kamkwamba

I want to build a machine that can drill wells for water. With this problem of water in many places in Africa, we need to find a solution for how you can dig wells so you can be pumping water from deeper places.

William Kamkwamba

Africa is on the rise.

Bill Gates

The Green Revolution focused on the big three - maize, rice and wheat - and the Green Revolution did not adapt the big three to African conditions, other than South Africa, as much as they should have.

Bill Gates

When I am in Africa, I always have the feeling that it's where everything started. When I am in New York, I know it is where everything ended up.

Henry Rollins

In my many trips to South Africa, I have met and spoken to a lot of people there, and they all seem to find apartheid as repellent as you would.

Henry Rollins

When a pile of cups is tottering on the edge of the table and you warn that they will crash to the ground, in South Africa you are blamed when that happens.

Desmond Tutu

Nelson Mandela will always be the face of South Africa. The traveler passing through the country will see Mandela's face almost everywhere he looks. Truly, the man is omnipresent.

Henry Rollins

I tell you, Bono may have a point. South Africa needs a Walmart.

Rush Limbaugh

Corruption is Africa's greatest problem. Not poverty. Not lack of riches. Not racism.

Dennis Prager

There was a time when all dark-skinned people were called Ethiopians, for the Greeks referred to Africa as, 'The Land Of The Burnt-Face People.'

John Henrik Clarke

Sub-Saharan Africa is also home to 400 million of the world's poorest people.

Bono

So you cannot, as a Christian, walk away from Africa.

Bono

Africa will thrive.

Bono

In many ways Africa subsidised America and Europe's development.

Jesse Jackson

It is important to nurture any new ideas and initiatives which can make a difference for Africa.

Wangari Maathai

I truly believe that when the history books are written, our age will be remembered for three things: the war on terror, the digital revolution, and what we did - or did not do - to put the fire out in Africa. History, like God, is watching what we do.

Bono

In Jamaica, we eradicated polio many years ago, but there are a lot of kids suffering in Africa still.

Ziggy Marley

I've been to North Africa many times.

Martin Scorsese

In Africa, those who have money - businessmen and banks - do not believe in film.

Wole Soyinka

If African countries can unite and pull resources together, then that will be the best thing we could ever do for the problems in Africa including AIDS.

Ziggy Marley

One of the things I love about Africa is the amount of dignity and respect and humility you see all the time. You don't realise how often you're disrespected until you are surrounded by respect.

Jill Scott

Contrasting sharply, in the developing countries represented by India, Pakistan, and most of the countries in Asia and Africa, seventy to eighty percent of the population is engaged in agriculture, mostly at the subsistence level.

Norman Borlaug

Africa is really a place for the wealthy traveler. It's got some nice hotels, but they're very expensive hotels. It doesn't really cater to the backpacker or to the overland traveler.

Paul Theroux

South Africa has all the tools to compete in the new global village - an eager workforce, ready to take on any challenge.

Tom Peters

It's important to debunk the myths of Africa being this benighted continent civilized only when white people arrived. In fact, Africans had been creators of culture for thousands of years before. These were very intelligent, subtle and sophisticated people, with organized societies and great art.

Henry Louis Gates

I've been working with Pat Robertson on Africa debt-relief, and we disagree on virtually everything except certain very specific, inalienable rights, and the truth is that morality and patriotism come in all shapes and sizes.

George Clooney

Africa has no future.

V. S. Naipaul

There are places that I've always wanted to go. First I went to Africa, and when I was there I realized there were places in Africa I really to wanted to visit: The Congo, West Africa, Mombassa. I wanted to see the deep, dark, outlandish places.

Paul Theroux

I had a hard time convincing students that they were going to North Africa to understand the North Africans, not to understand themselves.

Clifford Geertz

There has long been a debate in the aid community and in Africa about how to most effectively help situations of poverty in developing nations and underprivileged communities.

Marcus Samuelsson

In Africa through the 1990s, with notable exceptions in Senegal and Uganda, nearly all the ruling powers denied they had a problem with AIDS.

Barton Gellman

Most of the ancestors that I can trace were born here in the United States of America. And then it goes back to slavery. And I'm sure my ancestors go all the way back to Africa, but I feel more of an affinity for America than I do for Africa. I'm a black man in America.

Herman Cain

When diamonds' role in fuelling violent conflict in Africa gained worldwide attention, the diamond industry established the Kimberley process in order to keep "blood diamonds" out of international trade.

Peter Singer

You cannot blame the mismanagement of the economy or the fact that we have not invested adequately in education in order to give our people the knowledge, the skills and the technology that they need in order to be able to use the resources that Africa has to gain wealth.

Wangari Maathai

Multinationals don't pay taxes in Africa - we all know that.

Mo Ibrahim

I wanted to be a great white hunter, a prospector for gold, or a slave trader. But then, when I was eight, my parents sent me to a boarding school in South Africa. It was the equivalent of a British public school with cold showers, beatings and rotten food. But what it also had was a library full of books.

Wilbur Smith

If you wrote a novel in South Africa which didn't concern the central issues, it wouldn't be worth publishing.

Alan Paton

Africa has more dictators per capita than any other continent.

George Ayittey

Sinn Fein has productively taken the example of South Africa and, as we develop the peace process, we continue to use examples from South Africa.

Gerry Adams

A matter that seems to be very clear in terms of the alternative view, is what do you expect to happen in Africa with regard to immune systems, where people are poor, subject to repeat infections and all of that. Surely you would expect their immune systems to collapse.

Thabo Mbeki

The Western stereotype of Africa and its black citizens as devoid of reason and, therefore, subhuman was often shared by white master and black ex-slave alike.

Henry Louis Gates

It is wrong to divide the nation white against black, native born against immigrant or one religion against another. It is also wrong to divide people by income. East Germany was not an improvement over South Africa. Obama divides Americans against each other. This is wrong.

Grover Norquist

The solutions to Africa's problems lie in Africa, not in Live Aid concerts.

George Ayittey

I've always been fascinated by activists, people who will devote their life to a cause, people who go to India and to Africa and put their life in jeopardy to do what they believe is right.

Rachel Weisz

From Mozambique to Chad, South Africa and Liberia, Sierra Leone to Burkina Faso, feminism is the buzzword for a generation of women determined to change the course of the future for themselves and their families.

Mariella Frostrup

I love the sea as much as I love the veldt of Africa.

Wilbur Smith

And those Texas sunsets... I work a lot in Africa: Texas and Africa have the best sunsets on the planet, that I've ever seen.

Taylor Kitsch

Compared to people in Africa, I think we've all had privileged upbringings.

Julian Casablancas

Retail banking in Africa is very weak. You can't go to a village and get money from an ATM or visit a branch of the bank. So people have to use the Internet.

Mo Ibrahim

I am still a socialist. I am a left-of-center politician. I believe that in Africa, if you see the poverty around us, you can't afford to be anything else.

John Dramani Mahama

Africa is not a fun place, you know. A fun place is somewhere that lifts the spirits, that cossets the senses. I don't think that can be said of the Africa I traveled in.

V. S. Naipaul

I never set out to be a journalist. I wanted to be a humanitarian doctor like Albert Schweitzer, working in Africa.

Janine di Giovanni

The biggest opportunity in 2013 is in Africa. It has seven out of the ten fastest-growing economies in the world. In Nigeria alone there are 100 million people with mobile phones. In total, 300 million Africans - five times the population of Britain - are in the middle class.

David Miliband

In black Africa, one does not strike, one does not express, one walks right.

Yannick Noah

Every day, families in Africa go without food and water, never knowing when their next meal might be; but we can change that if we all work together. In order to make a difference, every purchase of my new energy shot, Street King, will provide a meal for a child in need.

Curtis Jackson

Many people say I smile more in Africa than in Sweden.

Henning Mankell

We tend to separate two crises going on in the same neighborhood, southern Europe's financial crisis and northern Africa's Arab Spring. Now that we have found new energy resources in this region, we can really develop green energy including solar and wind. Why not have a green Marshall Plan, which will bring in investments and stabilize the region.

George Papandreou

My work has been much more Caribbean and eclectic. I am interested in people, and where they come from happens to have fallen within an area of Africa.

Katherine Dunham

When I was doing 'Generation Kill' in Africa I worked with five really super-trained Navy SEALs who taught us all these moves like how to disarm people: if there's a bar fight and someone's got a chair or there's someone with a gun behind our head, how to disable them and take them down in a swift move.

Kellan Lutz

To all those who have drawn the inference from my words that Africa, as a continent, is somehow genetically inferior, I can only apologise unreservedly.

James D. Watson

Despite the fact that I spend a lot of time in London, Switzerland and New York, Africa is the place I know and love best, and my heart will always lie here.

Wilbur Smith

Rural communities in Africa, South Asia and Latin America are where the majority of hungry people are and the inequality that exists between women and men in these communities is holding back progress. These women have a very tough time, so much is expected of them.

Dionne Warwick

The Mormon mission to Africa, as to other dark-skinned parts of the world, was for a long time hobbled by the racism of the movement's scripture.

James Fenton

The biggest problem in South Africa is that we have a disrupted timeline. Historically, politically, spiritually, economically, in people's minds, in people's heads.

Abdullah Ibrahim

We view South Africa as one of our closest strategic partners in the developing world and in the African continent.

Pratibha Patil

Half of the hospital beds in sub-Saharan Africa are filled with people suffering from what are generally known as water-related diseases.

Rose George

There's a saying in Africa: 'To find out you are pregnant is to have one foot in the grave.'

Liya Kebede

In Africa, we have the bush meat trade, which means that, on a very large scale, animals are being killed in the forests and sold in the cities as a luxury food.

Frans de Waal

And I think that Africa is making progress that the world needs to recognize and assist the continent to continue on that path.

John Dramani Mahama

It's become relatively commonplace to find corners of Africa that have good cell coverage but no electrical power.

Ethan Zuckerman

All of our forebears contributed to what South Africa has become. That does not, however, mean that I must apologize to anyone for being born a Zulu, or for having that culture.

Mangosuthu Buthelezi

The givers of most of the corruption in Africa are from outside Africa.

Olusegun Obasanjo

If NATO goes in and solves the crisis in Darfur, when the next one comes along Africa's leaders will just sit back.

George Ayittey

In the West, the basic economic and social unit is the individual; in Africa, it is the extended family or the collective.

George Ayittey

Malaria is a disease that kills one to three million people a year. 300 to 500 million cases are reported. It's estimated that Africa loses about 13 billion dollars a year to the disease. Five dollars can save a life. We can send people to the moon; we can see if there's life on Mars - why can't we get five-dollar nets to 500 million people?

Jacqueline Novogratz

Music is something I must do, business is something I need to do, and Africa is something I have to do. That's the way it breaks down in my life.

Bob Geldof

As regards to personal safety, you do have to be careful not to put yourself at risk when travelling in South Africa. You don't want to go out exploring at night, for example.

Wilbur Smith

Many people have compared me to the Victorian adventure writer, Rider Haggard. I accept that as a compliment. As a boy growing up in Central Africa I read all Haggard's African novels.

Wilbur Smith

I have family members who live in Africa. Because of the family that lives there, I know what is happening in these countries, and it seems so silly to me that diseases like malaria are so prevalent when they are entirely preventable. Yet children are still dying every 35 seconds.

Katharine McPhee

I'm in awe of the AIDS workers in Africa who teach there, year in and year out.

Jordana Spiro

For me, personally, life in South Africa had come to an end. I had been lucky in some of the whites I had met. Meeting them had made a straight 'all-blacks-are-good, all-whites-are-bad' attitude impossible. But I had reached a point where the gestures of even my friends among the whites were suspect, so I had to go or be forever lost.

Peter Abrahams

Previous efforts to eradicate malaria failed for several reasons, including political instability and technical challenges in delivering resources, especially in certain countries in Africa.

Anthony Fauci

As far as those kinds of things, I also played at the concert to call for the release of Nelson Mandela when he was a political prisoner in South Africa. We were celebrating his 70th birthday and calling for his release.

Jackson Browne

Right now, the Anglo people are desperately trying to hold on to the United States, like they tried to hold on to Africa.

Edward James Olmos

Why would you want to go all the way to Africa and shoot a giraffe? I don't think you can eat him. I only shoot stuff I can eat.

Boo Weekley

When a woman has her first child in places like Africa, they're really young. They can be 12, 13,14, so their frames are really small, and they're usually malnourished.

Liya Kebede

Historically, epics are set in Africa or Asia or the Wild West, but if you make an epic today it's hard to disassociate from the contemporary realities of those places.

Baz Luhrmann

I had to inspect all fighter units in Russia, Africa, Sicily, France, and Norway. I had to be everywhere.

Adolf Galland

Reality shows that, contrary to other countries in southern Africa, we have no basis for a classical guerilla struggle. We have never had a hinterland, and we do not expect to.

Joe Slovo

People have an opinion of Africa and it is not so good, but we have to let sport unite us all.

Didier Drogba

In India there are more poor people in three states... than there are in the whole of sub-Saharan Africa.

Andrew Mitchell

The Cold War in Africa is one of the darkest, most disgraceful pages in contemporary history, and everybody ought to be ashamed.

Ryszard Kapuscinski

As a kid in Africa, you were so connected to nature itself because you went farming, watched the moon out at night, observed how the sky was different, and how the birds chanted different songs in the evening and the morning.

Ishmael Beah

We all have that capacity to lose our humanity when circumstances force us to do so. It's not specific to people who live in Africa or Latin America or Asia. And equally, we are capable of regaining ourselves.

Ishmael Beah

Any atrocity that's committed against one person affects us all, and we are becoming more of one society, of a global society, so something that happens in the Middle East or something that happens in Africa, something that happens in Asia, affects all of us.

Don Lemon

We must then build a proper relationship between the richest and the poorest countries based on our desire that they are able to fend for themselves with the investment that is necessary in their agriculture, so that Africa is not a net importer of food, but an exporter of food.

Gordon Brown

Novelists go about the strenuous business of marrying and burying their people, or else they send them to sea, or to Africa, or at the least, out of town. Essayists in their stillness ponder love and death.

Cynthia Ozick

South Africa is blessed to have women and men like yourselves who have little to give but give what you have with open hands and open hearts.

Mangosuthu Buthelezi

I've always thought that underpopulated countries in Africa are vastly underpolluted.

Lawrence Summers

Without white South Africa realizing what it had done - and on the basis of that realization having the courage to ask for forgiveness - there can really be no significant movement.

Athol Fugard

There was free trade in Africa. There was free enterprise in Africa before the colonialists came.

George Ayittey

Western-style multi-party democracy is possible but not suitable for Africa.

George Ayittey

Africa suffered under European dominance for centuries.

Jacob Zuma

The essence of Africa's crisis is fundamentally its extreme poverty.

Jeffrey Sachs

Nelson Mandela did much more than advocate the practice of democracy in South Africa. Working with a constitutional assembly that drew on the ideas and input of regional representatives as well as ordinary citizens, the president worked to draft a constitution that is now universally regarded as the most progressive of any in the world - bar none.

Aberjhani

The whole of that part of Southern Africa which is controlled by racial minorities is experiencing either consistent and regular guerilla activity or is faced with advanced preparation for its commencement.

Joe Slovo

In America there is a public library in every community. How many public libraries are there in Africa? Every day there are new books coming out and new ideas being discussed. But these new books and ideas don't reach Africa and we are being left behind.

George Weah

I can recognize the calls of practically every bird in North America. There are some in Africa I don't know, though.

Roger Tory Peterson

The Taliban, broadly speaking, are Afghans - farmers, subsistence farmers. As I say, most of those people can't find the United States on the map. Al Qaeda, traditionally, are much more educated, middle-class people, often from Egypt, from Saudi Arabia, North Africa.

Rory Stewart

With a tennis racket strapped tightly to her hiking pack, Martina Navratilova began her ascent of Mount

Kilimanjaro. The tennis legend had visions of celebrating at the summit of Africa's highest peak by hitting a couple balls to see how far they might fly in the thin air at 19,341 feet.

Don Yaeger

I realized that I was African when I came to the United States. Whenever Africa came up in my college classes, everyone turned to me. It didn't matter whether the subject was Namibia or Egypt; I was expected to know, to explain.

Chimamanda Ngozi Adichie

The World Health Organisation has a lot of its medical experts sitting in Geneva while hospitals in Africa have no drugs and desperate patients are forced to seek medication on the black market.

Pauline Hanson

Americans' perceptions of Africa remain rooted in troubling stereotypes of helplessness and perpetual crisis.

John Prendergast

I see courage everywhere I go in Africa.

John Prendergast

Although native Africans domesticated some plants in the Sahel and in Ethiopia and in tropical West Africa, they acquired valuable domestic animals only later, from the north.

Jared Diamond

In the developing world, it's about time that women are on the agenda. For instance, 80 percent of small-subsistence farmers in sub-Saharan Africa are women, and yet all the programs in the past were predominantly focused on men.

Melinda Gates

In Africa, listening is a guiding principle. It's a principle that's been lost in the constant chatter of the Western world, where no one seems to have the time or even the desire to listen to anyone else.

Henning Mankell

When I was a very young author, I knew I needed to build myself a tower outside of Europe. Like when you're a hunter, and build towers to watch the animals move. I knew I would never understand the world without that perspective. I came to Africa for that rational reason, although I love Mozambique now.

Henning Mankell

I have always thought that the rapid economic development of South Africa would in the long run prove to be incompatible with the government's racial policies, and recent events have tended to confirm my opinion.

Harry Oppenheimer

The World Health Organization did a world health report in 2006. In the whole world about 60 countries are in dire situation in terms of having enough doctors. And many of these countries are in Sub-Saharan Africa. You know, that part of the world alone needs one million doctors.

Margaret Chan

But what really excited me was the idea that humans had a tremendous pre-history that went back millions of years. I wanted to go to Africa to find some of these creatures.

Donald Johanson

When I go to Africa and spend more time there with people who are the least of the least, those in desperate situations, I am broken by it. But I also find people with so much more joy and freedom living with nothing than I see walking down the streets of my own community here in Tennessee.

Steven Curtis Chapman

Chief executives, who themselves own few shares of their companies, have no more feeling for the average stockholder than they do for baboons in Africa.

T. Boone Pickens

My 94-year-old grandmother has always been so inspiring to me. She is kind, smart, brave, and independent. After graduating number one in her medical school class at a time when it was extremely rare for women to attend medical school, she worked with the World Health Organization in North Africa to eradicate tuberculosis.

Kelsey Chow

Hip-hop in Africa has been very often a duplication of an American experience, but in a context that's totally alien to it.

K'naan

The only thing to be said for air travel is speed. It makes possible travel on a scale unimaginable before our present age. Between the ages of 20 and four-score I visited every country in Europe, all save two in Latin America, ditto in Africa, and most of Asia, not counting eight trips to Australia and 60 to the United States - all by air.

Paul Johnson

I first travelled to Africa at the end of 1996 and was immediately captivated. I had planned on a three-week trip, and I ended up staying two months.

Susan Minot

I grew up in a farm in South Africa and I was scouted there and they sent me to Europe. It's kind of been blessed, since then it happened all so fast.

Candice Swanepoel

Conditions were so hard. To send the news out, telex was the only means, but telex was very rare in Africa. So if somebody was flying to Europe, we gave him correspondence to send after he arrived.

Ryszard Kapuscinski

In my view, Africa's real problems are cultural.

Hugh Masekela

Reading the text of my blog itself is not really the interesting part. The exciting part is how the Internet allows me to be the eyes and ears for the people sending me postings from Africa.

Ethan Zuckerman

South Africa had a long record of studies in prehistory, going back to the end of the last century.

Louis Leakey

Long after this wonderful event in the Earth's history, when the human species was spread over a good deal of Asia, Europe, and Africa, migration to the American continents began in attempts to find new feeding grounds and unoccupied areas for hunting and fishing.

Harry Johnston

Living in South Africa has had a very profound impact on my career.

Gail Kelly

As a young woman, I attended Witwatersrand University in Johannesburg, South Africa, which was then not segregated. But I witnessed the weight of apartheid everywhere around me.

Teresa Heinz

You can make money, you can lose money in Africa. But opportunities, boy oh boy, they exist.

Euvin Naidoo

It was fortunate in looking back for South Africa and its entire people that Mandela and I found it possible to work together even though big strains developed between us from time to time.

F. W. de Klerk

Across Africa there is what I call a colonialist mentality or orthodoxy. Orthodoxy in the sense that a lot of things have gone wrong in Africa in the post-colonial period. And time and time again, any time something went wrong, the leadership claims that it was never their fault.

George Ayittey

In fact, a large majority of those have died and of those expected to die of AIDS, as well as of those who are infected with the virus, are in sub-Saharan Africa.

Claudio Hummes

South Africa is the most beautiful country I have been to. Canada is also hugely underrated.

Honor Blackman

That's why I felt so at home when I went to Africa. It didn't matter that I was halfway around the world in a foreign country, because all those elements are universal. And I think that's one thing about my work: It's universal.

Herb Ritts

The summer I finished my first novel 'Ghana Must Go,' I drove across west Africa: from Accra to Lome to Cotonou to the deliciously named Ouagadougou.

Taiye Selasi

People are beginning to understand there is nothing in the world so remote that it can't impact you as a person. It's not just diseases. Economists are now beginning to say if we are going to have good markets in Africa, we're going to have to have healthy people in Africa.

William Foege

The Internet is emblematic of an era in which what happens in Southeast Asia or southern Africa - from democratic advances to deforestation to the fight against aids - can affect Americans. As has been observed about water pollution, we all live downstream now.

Shashi Tharoor

This country is armed to the teeth, and none of these African states could begin to attack South Africa.

Helen Suzman

I see courage everywhere I go in Africa. Fearless human rights activists in Darfur. Women peace advocates in eastern Congo. Former child soldiers in Northern Uganda who now are helping other former child soldiers return to civilian life.

John Prendergast

Africa needs more funding to continue to fight all of those diseases. We are losing more than 1.3 million young children under the age of five every year because of malaria. We've already lost 25 million people to the pandemic of HIV-AIDS. More people are dying now from typhoid fever. Diabetes is on the rise.

Dikembe Mutombo

I always felt that I had to leave a legacy on the African continent. As I was only the third player to come to the NBA from Africa, I felt I had to do my best to recruit more young Africans to come and play in the NBA - and also find a way to bring the NBA to Africa.

Dikembe Mutombo

The problem with being a journalist is you go places and you're working. You don't get to appreciate everything. But I got enough of a sampler of South Africa; I thought, 'I want to come here when I don't have to interview people for a living so that I can really enjoy it.' Because I think it was just a magnificent place.

Lester Holt

All the rest of us - you and me and even the thousands of soldiers behind the lines in Africa - we want terribly yet only academically for the war to get over.

Ernie Pyle

For many, the icon of the British Museum is the Rosetta Stone, that administrative by-product of the Greek imperial adventure in Africa.

Neil MacGregor

If people in this country think of Africa as a place with kids and flies swarming around their heads, then they won't understand that these people are you and you are them.

Don Cheadle

Apartheid was in South Africa; now it has been transferred to Palestine.

Yahya Jammeh

The G8 nations, together with the five major emerging economies of China, India, South Africa, Brazil, Mexico, use almost three-quarters of the Earth's biocapacity - the capacity of the world's ecosystems to produce natural resources and to reduce harmful substances.

Sigmar Gabriel

The reason I'm in San Diego is not because I want distance from South Africa but because I want proximity to the people I love. But I don't envy growing up in America. As ugly as aspects of it were, my biggest blessing was to be born a South African.

Athol Fugard

I engaged upon those activities because I believed that, in the dangerous circumstances which have been created in South Africa, it was my duty to do so.

Bram Fischer

I certainly feel I'm carrying the flag for Britain. I feel an honour in that but, at the same time, knowing my roots are in Africa, I'd like that to help motivate people from there. Even coming from a third world country, it is possible to get to the top of wherever they want to be.

Chris Froome

To have been selected to represent Team South Africa at the London 2012 Olympic Games in the individual 400m and the 4x400m relay is a real honor and I am so pleased that years of hard work, determination and sacrifice have all come together.

Oscar Pistorius

Everything that the West is today is predominantly because of Africa.

Nneka

The fact that I have always been deeply invested in politics, and African politics in particular, inevitably played a role in my first novel and, of course, in my decision to write about a handful of particular conflicts in Africa as a journalist.

Dinaw Mengestu

When I began 'All Our Names,' I did so wanting to create parallel narratives between Africa in the nineteen-seventies and America during that same period.

Dinaw Mengestu

That the AIDS pandemic is threatening sustainable development in Africa only reinforces the reality that health is at the center of sustainable development.

Gro Harlem Brundtland

Women in Africa, generally a lot needs to be done for women. Women are not being educated, not only in Angola but my trip to Nigeria, one point I would make over and over again was that women need to be educated too.

Mia Farrow

I think that Africa has made quite rapid progress and a lot of the conflicts that we saw on the continent have abated.

John Dramani Mahama

Inspiration, in its rich variety, must be present in any discussion about Africa. We need role models - they are essential to the advancement of our society.

Richard Attias

When I left South Africa in 1960 I was 20 years old. I wanted to try to get an education, and music education was not available for me in South Africa.

Hugh Masekela

When I left South Africa there were 10 million people - when I came back there were more than 40 million. I had to learn how to get to the highways because when I left where there were no highways.

Hugh Masekela

There are, of course, all sorts of other unpleasant regimes outside the walls as well - the military dictators of Latin America and the apartheid regime of South Africa.

Barbara Amiel

Improving Africa's farming sector would have multiple positive outcomes for African people.

Richard Attias

The event of the landing of these brethren upon our shores is to be, not without its beneficial effect, as well to the colored population of this country, as it promises to be to ill-fated Africa.

Lewis Tappan

My Mother was a very wild Australian woman. When we were in Africa she could kill a snake with one blow from a crow bar, which she kept at the back door.

Mem Fox

I hope more people will ask diamond companies to continue changing the way they do business in Africa.

Djimon Hounsou

The question of modernization is central to disturbances in the Middle East and in Africa. Everyone is after modernization, no matter where they come from. But you have to be careful about it, and more importantly, you have to have sense about it.

Youssou N'Dour

Sometime during the many millions of years that have elapsed since mammalian faunas came into existence, some sort of island crossed from West Africa to South America.

Louis Leakey

All I know is that every time I go to Africa, I am shaken to my core.

Stephen Lewis

It gives one hope, this great strength of Africa.

Stephen Lewis

There's a false perception that women in Africa somehow don't love their babies they way we do, don't grieve their loss the way we would. That is simply not true.

Melinda Gates

Aside from all that, we recall that antibodies to malaria and other diseases prevalent in Africa show up as HIV-positive on tests.

Serge Lang

With my government, we engaged in bringing our help to fights for national freedom. At that precise moment, several countries were still colonised or had barely overcome colonisation. This was the case in practically all of Africa. We supported them.

Ahmed Ben Bella

It makes it difficult to decide which to go see, since no film about say, some tragic genocide in Africa is going to get a bad review even if it's poorly made.

Terry Zwigoff

Lebanon, Israel, Ireland, South Africa - wherever there is a bleeding sore on the body of the world, the same hard-eyed narrow-minded fanatics are busy, indifferent to life, in love with death.

J. M. Coetzee

I profess accurately to describe native Africa - Africa in those places where it has not received the slightest impulse, whether for good or evil, from European civilisation.

John Hanning Speke

I was afterwards sorry for this, though, if I ever travel again, I shall trust to none but natives, as the climate of Africa is too trying to foreigners.

John Hanning Speke

Yeah, my dad was in the foreign service. We lived in India, Indonesia and Africa, and we traveled a lot from those places. I was 10 when we moved back, and I felt like the odd guy out. It wasn't until later that I appreciated it. But coming back I didn't know any TV shows or music, which was even worse.

Dylan Walsh

I was in Africa once. I was in Kenya. I got off the plane, and I thought, 'Africa...' Some guy in a dashiki said, 'Mr. Bundy. Oh my God, it's you.'

Ed O'Neill

Sometimes, you'll watch the news and you'll see two-year-old boys in South Africa, wearing 'Spider-Man' t-shirts. It's such a global phenomenon.

James Vanderbilt

Women account for about 70% of Africa's food production and manage a large proportion of small enterprises. They are also increasingly represented in legislative and executive leadership positions.

Ngozi Okonjo-Iweala

Africa is the most weathered continent in the world; 75 percent of its soil has been degraded. You don't just bring that back. I always like to say it's like putting an oxygen mask on a cadaver; it just isn't going to work.

Howard Graham Buffett

You've got a global food problem. You've got a food problem in the United States. You've got a food problem in Africa... in Asia. And so the truth is, the U.S. is going to have to produce more, on not very many more acres, honestly. And so we're going to have to do a better job.

Howard Graham Buffett

Africa is a continent in flames. And deep down, if we really accepted that Africans were equal to us, we would all do more to put the fire out. We're standing around with watering cans, when what we really need is the fire brigade.

Bono

I came back from university thinking I knew all about politics and racism, not knowing my dad had been one of the youngest-serving Labour councillors in the town and had refused to work in South Africa years ago because of the situation there. And he's never mentioned it - you just find out. That's a real man to me. A sleeping lion.

Johnny Vegas

If the United States of America or Britain is having elections, they don't ask for observers from Africa or from Asia. But when we have elections, they want observers.

Nelson Mandela

The global phenomenon of poverty tourism - or 'poorism' -
has become increasingly popular during the past few years.
Tourists pay to be guided through the favelas of Brazil and
the shantytowns of South Africa. The recently opened Los
Angeles Gang Tour carries visitors through battle-scarred
territories of urban violence and deprivation.

Leslie Jamison

What should we suppose must naturally be the consequence
of our carrying on a slave trade with Africa? With a
country, vast in its extent, not utterly barbarous, but
civilized in a very small degree? Does any one suppose a
slave trade would help their civilization?

William Wilberforce

There are many people in South Africa who are rich and
who can share those riches with those not so fortunate who
have not been able to conquer poverty.

Nelson Mandela

If I read not amiss, this powerful race will move down upon
Mexico, down upon Central and South America, out upon
the islands of the sea, over upon Africa and beyond. And

can any one doubt that the results of this competition of races will be the 'survival of the fittest?'

Josiah Strong

We believe that the world, too, can destroy apartheid, firstly by striking at the economy of South Africa.

Oliver Tambo

At the outset, I want to say that the suggestion that the struggle in South Africa is under the influence of foreigners or communists is wholly incorrect. I have done whatever I did because of my experience in South Africa and my own proudly felt African background, and not because of what any outsider might have said.

Nelson Mandela

In time, we shall be in a position to bestow on South Africa the greatest possible gift - a more human face.

Steven Biko

You have to realize that up until about 1959, Africa was dominated by the colonial powers. And by the colonial powers of Europe having complete control over Africa, they projected Africa always in a negative light - jungles, savages, cannibals, nothing civilized.

Malcolm X

This world was not created piecemeal. Africa was born no later and no earlier than any other geographical area on this globe. Africans, no more and no less than other men, possess all human attributes, talents and deficiencies, virtues and faults.

Haile Selassie

So what we're talking about here is human rights. The right to live like a human. The right to live, period. And what we're facing in Africa is an unprecedented threat to human dignity and equality.

Bono

Thousands of years ago, civilizations flourished in Africa which suffer not at all by comparison with those of other continents. In those centuries, Africans were politically free and economically independent. Their social patterns were their own and their cultures truly indigenous.

Haile Selassie

All these boundaries - Africa, Asia, Malaysia, America - are set by men. But you don't have to look at boundaries when you are looking at a man - at the character of a man. The question is: What do you stand for? Are you a follower, or are you a leader?

Hakeem Olajuwon

I would say colonialism is a wonderful thing. It spread civilization to Africa. Before it they had no written language, no wheel as we know it, no schools, no hospitals, not even normal clothing.

Ian Smith

I know no national boundary where the Negro is concerned. The whole world is my province until Africa is free.

Marcus Garvey

Let there be an end to the arrogance of the big powers who miss no opportunity to put the rights of the people in question. Africa's absence from the club of those who have the right to veto is unjust and should be ended.

Thomas Sankara

My favourite animal is the koala, but his life would be boring. I would rather be a giraffe so that I could contemplate the beauty of Africa.

Caterina Murino

I have been to the Occupied Palestinian Territory, and I have witnessed the racially segregated roads and housing that reminded me so much of the conditions we experienced in South Africa under the racist system of Apartheid.

Desmond Tutu

Turkey is a European country, an Asian country, a Middle Eastern country, Balkan country, Caucasian country, neighbor to Africa, Black Sea country, Caspian Sea, all these.

Ahmet Davutoglu

When I look back over my life it's almost as if there was a plan laid out for me - from the little girl who was so passionate about animals who longed to go to Africa and whose family couldn't afford to put her through college. Everyone laughed at my dreams. I was supposed to be a secretary in Bournemouth.

Jane Goodall

I'd like to one day be featured on a list of inspirational people who have made a difference in the world, whether it be helping underprivileged people or putting an end to the poaching of wildlife in Africa.

Candice Swanepoel

In Africa today, we recognise that trade and investment, and not aid, are pillars of development.

Paul Kagame

For all its problems, I found South Africa a beautiful country, interesting and inspiring.

David Harewood

I'm extremely optimistic about rapid transformation and change of things in Africa in general.

Binyavanga Wainaina

Living in South Africa and periodically coming back to Kenya, my relationship with officialdom in Kenya was just insane.

Binyavanga Wainaina

The factors that have been holding farmers back are similar to those that threaten other types of growth in Africa. Infrastructure and transport are in many cases quite poor, resulting in the losses of huge amounts of produce.

Richard Attias

I believe education should be a right for every child, but tragically in many parts of world it is a privilege for certain children whose parents have money. There are 72 million children in the world who don't go to school and many of them are in Africa.

George Weah

It turns out that every person alive today can trace his or her ancestry back to Africa. Everyone's DNA tells a story of a journey from an African homeland to wherever you live.

Spencer Wells

America has this understanding of Africans that plays like National Geographic: a bunch of Negroes with loincloths running around the plain fields of Africa chasing gazelles.

Djimon Hounsou

I think it is very ironic that most people think that the banjo is a southern white instrument. It came from Africa and even for the first years that white people played banjo they would put on blackface.

Bela Fleck

I think when you've travelled around a lot in Africa, you understand something that many people here don't recognize: the extraordinary power that is Africa at village level - at community level.

Stephen Lewis

I mean enormous pressure was brought to bear - Valerie Amos, Lady Amos, went round Africa with people from our intelligence services trying to press them. I had to make sure that we didn't promise a misuse of aid in a way that would be illegal.

Clare Short

An Obama administration truly looking to break with the molds of the past would stop treating Africa as an obligation and start treating it as globalization's next great opportunity, understanding that Chinese - along with Indians and Arab sovereign wealth funds - are natural partners in this process.

Thomas P.M. Barnett

I was with a folk trio back in '63 and '64, and we traveled all across North Africa, Israel, and Europe.

Creed Bratton

Most of the Amazon basin is as flat as a pancake and laced with extravagantly meandering waterways. One school of thought holds that more than 145 million years ago, when Africa and South America were joined, the Amazon's main stem was connected to the Niger River and actually flowed in the opposite direction, toward the Pacific Ocean.

Alex Shoumatoff

Ninety-nine percent of Americans have never had malaria, but I've been in Africa and have had malaria six times, so I can say now what it's like to get malaria, and it's horrible.

Bruce Wilkinson

If it were in our national security to deploy to South Africa under apartheid, would we have found it acceptable or customary to segregate African American soldiers from other American soldiers, and say, 'It's just a cultural thing'? I don't think so. I would hope not.

Martha McSally

I am no fashion diva - I grew up on the beaches in South Africa and am a nature girl that spends a lot of time outdoors. Fashion speaks to me through an occasion.

Tanit Phoenix

Beyond the borders of wealthy countries like the United States, in developing countries where most people in the world live, the impacts of climate change are much more deadly, from the growing desertification of Africa to the threats of rising sea levels and the submersion of small island nations.

Amy Goodman

I have never collected an object or figure from Africa or Oceania because of anything curious about it or because of its utility or historic interest. Everything has been chosen entirely because of its aesthetic significance; its form, feeling, structure, and plastic values.

Frank Crowninshield

I suppose if I were younger, I would be investing in Africa.

Julian Robertson

You eat a lot of goat stomach when you're in North Africa. You eat whatever's put in front of you. I am a big proponent of that.

Ronan Farrow

I don't think anyone who has been to Africa comes away untouched by the place. You see a lot of beauty and optimism, but you also come away with an awareness of the huge gulf between what most of us have and what most of them have to make do with. Then, every now and then, a famine or a war makes everything a hundred times worse.

Gary Frank

In South Africa, where HIV-positive children are often shunned, we have an HIV-positive Muppet to teach children to be friendly with children with HIV. But they use local actors. And it's not always a street. Sometimes it's 'Sesame Plaza,' or 'Sesame Tree.'

Joan Ganz Cooney

The first breath of air of Africa - it felt like you were in another continent - you were, you were - and it was different.

Romeo Dallaire

I don't see why OPEC countries should continue to cut production just to keep the price of oil high. This will not affect the industrial countries alone, it will also hit poor countries in Africa, Asia and Latin America. Who will look after them?

Hamad bin Khalifa Al Thani

South Africa is a whole other world. I went to grade school there and high school in Johannesburg, and before that, my family lived in Kenya in Nairobi where my brother was actually born, and my sister was born in Capetown. I spent the first 10 years of my life in South Africa.

Jann Klose

I would love to do a film in Africa.

Judi Shekoni

Whether I'm trying to figure out what the U.S. military is doing in Latin America or Africa, Afghanistan or Qatar, the response is remarkably uniform - obstruction and obfuscation, hurdles and hindrances. In short, the good old-fashioned military runaround.

Nick Turse

What offends me the most when I hear criticisms about this so-called Africa bias is how quick we are to focus on the words and propaganda of a few powerful, influential individuals, and to forget about the millions of anonymous people who suffer from their crimes.

Fatou Bensouda

There were times when there were riots in Africa, demonstrations against the IMF because of the policy advice they were giving, the conditionalities they were imposing, and the difficulties that arose out of the implementation of those conditionalities.

Jakaya Kikwete

The very first role I ever played was as a 17-year old South African girl who dreamed of being a star and left home to meet her mother in the big city so that she could pursue that dream. I left South Africa and met my mother in Vancouver and not long after that was given the opportunity to perform on the stage and have people chant my name.

Kandyse McClure

You have to remember that although Gandhi and Churchill only met physically once, their paths crossed again and crossed again all over the globe, from London and South Africa and India and back to London. In fact, I discovered that during the Boer War in 1899 they literally passed yards from each other on the battlefield.

Arthur L. Herman

The majority of small-holder farmers in Africa are women and, in urban areas, you're primarily looking at women-led households. So we can't solve hunger if we don't have gender-sensitive programming that addresses access to opportunities for women, whether it's through education or tools for cooking, like solar-powered stoves.

Ertharin Cousin

I grew up in Africa surrounded by a lot of culture. It's made me aware that the world is a big place.

Jann Klose

When Europeans first came to Africa, they considered the architecture very disorganized and thus primitive. It never occurred to them that the Africans might have been using a form of mathematics that they hadn't even discovered yet.

Ron Eglash

The first Western attempt to save Africa from itself was in the late 19th century. It was led by Christian missionaries who claimed to be seeking to end poverty, disease and the slave trade.

Andrew Mwenda

I grew up in South Africa without a television; there was no television, and the year after I left, television arrived in South Africa, so I have never really acquired a taste for watching television.

Alice Krige

Wherever I've been, and I've been to over 20, maybe 25, countries in Africa, I've noticed how their backbone is broken. They don't have any confidence in themselves.

They always think a white man will solve their problems from outside for them.

Bunker Roy

If I hadn't left South Africa, I felt I was at risk of being pigeonholed. I looked around and saw actors who, 10 to 15 years into their careers, were still playing stereotypical Afrikaans characters, stereotyped Indian characters. That was not something that I wanted for myself.

Adhir Kalyan

Remember, we really grew up separately; our life experience was very different because of segregation. So I think comedy is a good space to work those things out and educate everyone about the different experiences and different race groups in South Africa.

Riaad Moosa

We need self-confidence in our ability to build Africa. I trust in Mali and I trust in music.

Rokia Traore

I'm in 'Madagascar 2.' I'm Testy the Lion. The franchise moves to Africa, and Bernie Mac is also in the film. I loved working for Dreamworks on that film.

Tom Lister, Jr.

Global capital is agnostic - it has no loyalties. There's an overhang of capital in the U.S., and the key is yield pickup. What Africa is providing is a diversification play and also opportunities for yield pickup for the investor that's aware of what he or she is doing.

Euvin Naidoo

I spent seven months in Africa and came back saying there isn't anything you can say about black people that you couldn't say about, say, pink people except that they're black.

Larry Rivers

Islamic fundamentalism in its activist manifestation is bad news. Religious fundamentalism in general is bad news. We know about religious fundamentalism in South Africa. Calvinist fundamentalism has been an unmitigated force of benightedness in our history.

J. M. Coetzee

Politicians are easy to attack, but frankly, we are all guilty of not meeting the needs of Africa's young people properly.

Ama Ata Aidoo

The strange thing about Africa is how past, present and future come together in a kind of rough jazz, if you like.

Ben Okri

I fell in love with Africa and began helping people fix things there.

Martha Beck

The Sudanese government has been playing games with the world, with the Africa Union, in particular, have been playing for time in order to conclude its mission of ethnic cleansing in the Sudan.

Wole Soyinka

I love Bono. I really respect what he has done for Africa and how he has used his fame to do good in the world. I hope I can do half as much in my life.

Alicia Keys

I'm not pessimistic about Africa. The cities just seem big and hopeless. But there's still a great green heart where there's possibility. There's hope in the wilderness.

Paul Theroux

I grew up in South Africa and I would look at maps and we were at the bottom of the world. There was this whole thing up there. I was always reading encyclopedias about the world. So travel was something I was always attracted to.

Charlize Theron

The thing about Hemingway that people forget is that all the stuff he did was at a time where people weren't traveling that much. At 19 he travels to Italy. He goes to the Spanish Civil War. He goes to China, he goes to Africa so at that time to travel that much is really incredible.

Clive Owen

I don't think that anyone seriously fears that the world can be blown to pieces all together. But what one can fear and rightly so are regional things, like in the Middle East, India, Pakistan, the Korean Peninsula, borders in Africa, etc.

Hans Blix

The media in America is not covering American AIDS very much. They're covering African AIDS as if somehow miraculously it's all stopped here. Well, it hasn't, and the one thing they're not saying about Africa is that all those people are going to die; there's no way these people can be saved - none.

Larry Kramer

I am consciously not trying to bring in World Music elements. The ways that I work and feel are completely different in how they sound than someone playing the Kora in Africa would play it.

Joanna Newsom

In Africa... age is not important over there. They don't care.

Akon

So this is why I'm always say happy that somebody mentions Rwanda, because behind Rwanda, we have Africa.

Boutros Boutros-Ghali

This is my first opportunity to visit this part of North Africa, so I am going to be able to go back home and talk about this beautiful country and encourage Americans to travel here.

Donald Evans

The history of apartheid-era South Africa is incredibly sad and at times infuriatingly incomprehensible.

Henry Rollins

When I am in Africa, I realize I don't know much, have not seen much, and there's a lot to be done.

Henry Rollins

When I visit my brother in South Africa, I order things I've only seen in zoos. Little deers and kudu, all the mammals you would never think of eating.

Chuck Palahniuk

George W. Bush is very popular in Sub-Saharan Africa. Why? Because of PEPFAR, the President's Emergency Program for AIDS Relief.

Hillary Clinton

Africans who immigrate to America know how little racism exists there. They suspect it before emigrating from Africa, and they know it after arriving in America. Indeed, America, the Left's depiction of it notwithstanding, is the least racist country in the world.

Dennis Prager

Perhaps the great American Republic, whose interests lie in the Pacific and who has no hand in the spoliation of Africa, may someday dream of foreign possession.

Jose Rizal

I was learning to track rhinoceroses in Africa and tracked right up on an animal that really I thought was going to kill me.

Martha Beck

I have a daughter and two grand-daughters and a great grandson in Africa, in Cape Town.

Doris Lessing

I've been in Africa, America, moving around a lot. It's helped me to open up my mind. I was born in Jamaica; I've lived all my life there and got all I could from Jamaica. But I needed to be somewhere else to grow.

Ziggy Marley

Egypt was - as it is now - a confluence of cultures, as a result of being a crossroads geographically between Africa, the Middle East and Europe.

Ridley Scott

When I went to Africa, I was reduced to floods of tears every day.

Madonna Ciccone

In sub-Saharan Africa, fewer than 1 in 5 girls make it to secondary school.

Nancy Gibbs

Africa the continent is not just what we see on the news. It's... not AIDS, and it's not just war and poverty. It's so much more. It's an abundant continent, and Botswana is an abundant place.

Jill Scott

When I left Africa in 1966 it seemed to me to be a place that was developing, going in a particular direction, and I don't think that is the case now. And it's a place where people still kid themselves - you know, in a few years this will happen or that will happen. Well, it's not going to happen. It's never going to happen.

Paul Theroux

That is not enough. Sport has been great for me, a great learning place that if you want to achieve you can, even if you are from the poorest part of Africa.

Haile Gebrselassie

The idea of traveling in Africa for me is based on going by road or train or bus or whatever and crossing borders. You can't travel easily or at all through some countries.

Paul Theroux

It's a melting pot, southern Africa. You find these cultural collisions that result in art and music, and it's pretty amazing.

Dave Matthews

The Sahara is Africa's great divide.

Richard Engel

In Africa, the rangers shoot poachers.

Paul Watson

I knew that there were black people in Africa, of course, unfortunately because of movies such as 'Tarzan.'

Henry Louis Gates

In two years, there were 22 military coups d'etat, essentially in Africa and the third world. The coup d'etat of Algiers, in 1965, is what opened the path.

Ahmed Ben Bella

If I were to live in Africa, serving the poor, the number-one thing I'd miss wouldn't be running water or electricity - it would be style... being able to get dressed up and feel beautiful.

Evangeline Lilly

Africa has 53 countries. And you find that three or four countries in these 53 are dominating the news.

Mo Ibrahim

Africa is rich, and why are we poor then if our continent is rich. It is not right.

Mo Ibrahim

Africa is underpopulated. We have 20% of the world's landmass and 13% of its population.

Mo Ibrahim

Africa offers the highest return on investment in the world.

Mo Ibrahim

Africa should not again face isolation or stigmatisation based on ignorance and unrepresentative imagery.

Mo Ibrahim

Africa was perceived - it still is to some extent - as a place which is very difficult to do business in. I don't share that view.

Mo Ibrahim

All we hear about Africa in the West is Darfur, Zimbabwe, Congo, Somalia, as if that is all there is.

Mo Ibrahim

Almost every country in Africa has now instituted multi-party democracy.

Mo Ibrahim

Celtel established a mobile phone network in Africa at a time when investors told me that there was no market for mobile phones there.

Mo Ibrahim

Computers are very expensive and they need power, and that can be a problem in Africa.

Mo Ibrahim

I don't subscribe to the narrative that Africa is backward because of colonialism.

Mo Ibrahim

I think the Cold War was worse for Africa than colonialism.

Mo Ibrahim

I'm uncomfortable, frankly, with the hype about Africa. We went from one extreme... to, like, Africa now is the best thing after sliced bread.

Mo Ibrahim

If economic progress is not translated into better quality of life and respect for citizens' rights, we will witness more Tahrir Squares in Africa.

Mo Ibrahim

In a world of growing food demand, Africa is home to two-thirds of the world's unexploited arable land.

Mo Ibrahim

It was a no-brainer that the cellular route would be a great success in Africa.

Mo Ibrahim

It's time Africa started listening to our young people instead of always telling them what to do.

Mo Ibrahim

Mobile phones could not work in Africa without prepaid because it's a cash society.

Mo Ibrahim

Most of the money I made has gone back to Africa or is going back to Africa.

Mo Ibrahim

Nobody can come and develop Africa on behalf of Africans.

Mo Ibrahim

Nobody in Africa loves to be a beggar or a recipient of aid. Everywhere I go in Africa, people say, 'When are we going to stand up on our feet?'

Mo Ibrahim

Not any amount of aid is going to move Africa forward.

Mo Ibrahim

Roads are not practical in Africa.

Mo Ibrahim

The brain drain from Africa has been reversed.

Mo Ibrahim

The mobile industry changed Africa.

Mo Ibrahim

The U.S. has been a great friend all these years, but as soon as Africa found itself starting to move up, the U.S. is really disengaging.

Mo Ibrahim

The way forward for Africa is investment.

Mo Ibrahim

There is a crisis of leadership and governance in Africa, and we must face it.

Mo Ibrahim

To be frank, I don't think President Obama gives much thought to Africa - or gives much to Africa.

Mo Ibrahim

Transfer pricing is causing huge problems in Africa.

Mo Ibrahim

When you ask people what they think of Africa, they think of AIDS, genocide, disasters, famine.

Mo Ibrahim

Women in Africa are really the pillar of the society, are the most productive segment of society, actually. They do agriculture.

Mo Ibrahim

You fly for hours and hours and hours over Africa to go from one place to another.

Mo Ibrahim

I thought 'Out of Africa' would be a beautiful ballet.

Amy Adams

I go back to South Africa at least once a year, sometimes twice, and usually for a month. And probably, I'm guessing, I'll spend more time back there as I get older.

Dave Matthews

Drug manufacturers could afford to sell AIDS drugs in Africa at virtually any discount. The companies said they did not do so because Africa lacked the requisite infrastructure.

Barton Gellman

We can't stop a baby in Africa from starving to death... but we can afford enough technology and weaponry to blow the world up a million times over.

Paul Weller

When you look at - when you talk to people in Africa and across the Middle East, they're not satisfied with the way things are going. Sure, this idea of democracy was injected into the region, but it has brought mostly chaos.

Richard Engel

It is very much the theme of our President, President Thabo Mbeki, whose passion is for Africa to work together, and for Africans to get up and do things for us. We are trying as women to do things for ourselves.

Miriam Makeba

If China's expansion into Africa and Russia's into Latin America and the former Soviet Union are any indication, Silicon Valley's ability to expand globally will be severely limited, if only because Beijing and Moscow have no qualms about blending politics and business.

Evgeny Morozov

A narrative that branded Africa as little more than an economic, political and social basket case was not likely to provide the investment needed to drive development.

Mo Ibrahim

Africa is progressing but maybe not in the way you think it is. Even if the overall picture looks good, we must all remain vigilant and not get complacent.

Mo Ibrahim

Africa's success stories are delivering the whole range of the public goods and services that citizens have a right to

expect and are forging a path that we hope more will
follow.

Mo Ibrahim

Compared to developed countries, or even to some major
emerging countries, burdened by aging populations,
financial crises, widening budget deficits, faltering faith in
politics and growing social demands, Africa has become
the world's last 'New Frontier:' a kind of 'it-continent.'

Mo Ibrahim

Educational opportunities have supported the rise of the
African middle class, the professional cadre of young
people who are now willing and able to contribute to
Africa's future prosperity.

Mo Ibrahim

Everywhere in Africa, you see Indian, Chinese, Brazilian
businesses. Other than Coca Cola and the oil companies, it
is very rare to see American businesses.

Mo Ibrahim

Far from being hopeless, Africa is full of hope and potential, maybe more so than any other continent. The challenge is to ensure that its potential is utilised.

Mo Ibrahim

Increasing extremism - across Africa and the world - must be understood in the context of the failure of our leaders properly to manage diversity within their borders.

Mo Ibrahim

Of course, Nelson Mandela, everybody knows Nelson Mandela. I mean, he's a great gift not only for Africa but for the whole world, actually. But do not expect everybody to be a Nelson Mandela.

Mo Ibrahim

Sudan has been an experiment that resonated across Africa: if we, the largest country on the continent, reaching from the Sahara to the Congo, bridging religions, cultures and a multitude of ethnicities, were able to construct a prosperous and peaceful state from our diverse citizenry, so too could the rest of Africa.

Mo Ibrahim

What we need in Africa is balanced development.
Economic success cannot be a replacement for human
rights or participation or democracy... it doesn't work.

Mo Ibrahim

Culture constitutes an essential element of social and
political liberation. As people rise up across the Middle
East and North Africa, the diversity of their cultures is not
only the means but also the ultimate goal of their liberation
and their freedom.

Tariq Ramadan

Of course, with well-masticated food playing the role of
social glue, it's absolutely essential that everyone clear their
plate. Sod the starving kiddies in Africa - it's the overfed
ones here we need to worry about.

Will Self

To this day the Arab influence is evident in southern Italy,
northern Africa and, above all, in Spain.

Carroll Quigley

Africa is a very dangerous place.

Janine di Giovanni

I started writing an album on flights to Africa and Brazil, but it was crazy because I left the notebook on the plane. It had seven or eight songs in it. After that, I'm not writing any more songs on notebooks - and I keep my Blackberry close!

Estelle

First, I was opposed to gay marriage because it seemed like one more way that gays were wanting to assimilate. When I realized the Christian right was so opposed to it, as well as tyrannical governments in Africa and Russia, I thought, 'It must be a good thing to fight for.'

Edmund White

They say if you drink Zambezi water with your mother's milk, you are always a slave of Africa, and I am.

Wilbur Smith

I always dreamed when I was a little girl interested in animals that I would go live in Africa. Then I found out that you can look in your backyard, and you can do your own safari.

Isabella Rossellini

So the experts think we could have an AIDS-free generation in Africa by 2015, even if the mothers are positive.

Alan Cumming

Africa was the most exotic place I could conceive of - the end of the world - and I knew I would go there one day.

Henning Mankell

I love Africa.

Naomie Harris

Herbert, my father, was born in Britain but went out to Africa in his teens to join his father and built up an 18,000-acre ranch in what was then Northern Rhodesia, providing work for the locals. He was my hero when I was a boy.

Wilbur Smith

I read all of Rider Haggard's books. For me he had the romance of Africa with a little bit of mysticism. I'm delighted to be looked on as his heir and be categorised as an adventure novelist because that's exactly what I am.

Wilbur Smith

What is happening in the Sahel for the past several months is that terrorists have structured themselves, have installed themselves. It's not simply a menace for west Africa.

Francois Hollande

In Africa, you know, if you're poor, at least you can go to the forest and share some mangoes with the gorillas and monkey.

Emmanuel Jal

I was actually away in Africa doing 'Generation Kill' while everyone was auditioning for Twilight. They all had, like, five different auditions: I was so lucky that I came back from Africa just in time and the actor who was playing Emmett fell through, lucky for me!

Kellan Lutz

I must say the idea of a United Africa was nonsense.

C. L. R. James

But since independence, Gabon is one of the few countries in Central Africa that enjoys peace and stability.

Omar Bongo

Certainly, Africa accounts for only 1 % of world trade, and we cannot assure our development on our own.

Omar Bongo

Africa's salvation doesn't lie in begging and begging for more aid, and as an African, I find it very, very humiliating.

George Ayittey

I never think of playing for South Africa. It's the furthest thing from my mind.

Kevin Pietersen

I'm not your expert on Africa or animals or whatever. I'm not a travel writer or maker of documentaries. I was someone who doesn't know very much, trying to communicate.

Michael Palin

The United States is the most powerful nation on Earth and it just can't walk away from the Middle East and central Asia and the Horn of Africa.

John Abizaid

What you and I understand as a government doesn't exist in many African countries. In fact, what we call our governments are vampire states. Vampires because they suck the economic vitality out of their people. Government is the problem in Africa.

George Ayittey

I've been lucky to travel through quite a bit of Europe and Australia, but I would love to do Asia and South America and South Africa.

Dianna Agron

As a man may know about Africa either by going there personally or by reading descriptions written by travelers who have been there, so may he visit the super-physical realms if he will but qualify himself therefor, or he may learn what others who have so qualified themselves report as a result of their investigations.

Max Heindel

When the slaves left Africa, they left us this music. They left us blues.

Youssou N'Dour

Look at the history of peace accords in Africa. They have a terrible record. They are shredded even before the ink on them is dry.

George Ayittey

Leaving South Africa was very difficult.

Kevin Pietersen

I never thought I'd be comfortable living outside South Africa, but we love London. Our two kids were born here.

Ernie Els

In 2002, the 2000 Engelbrecht Els wine was released in South Africa and received high ratings.

Ernie Els

I've been able to look at the world differently from three continents practically. I've always lived between India and the U.S. When I married Mahmood I became a daughter-in-law of Africa. That really changed my worldview. I can see it from so many perspectives.

Mira Nair

I'm over there filming in South Africa now, and two in five are HIV-positive now. Not many people know that.

Bruce Davison

All across Africa, the Pacific and the Americas, we find cultures that didn't know about mouth kissing until their first contact with European explorers. And the attraction was not always immediately apparent. Most considered the act of exchanging saliva revolting.

Joshua Foer

I know everything about candy. Would you believe I even know where to find gumballs in the middle of Africa?

Dylan Lauren

I was a news reporter for 16 years, seven of them a foreign correspondent in the Middle East, Africa and the Balkans. Perhaps the most useful equipment I acquired in that time is a lack of preciousness about the act of writing. A reporter must write. There must be a story. The mot juste unarriving? Tell that to your desk.

Geraldine Brooks

I'd love to do a safari holiday somewhere in Africa - maybe Kenya or Tanzania. I have never been, and we've deliberately waited until the children are older so that they could appreciate it, learn something and come back with stories.

Louise Nurding

Just going to Africa is amazing; it all comes back to the motherland. It's pretty much where everything started.

Amar'e Stoudemire

I set up a laboratory in the Department of Physiology in the Medical School in South Africa and begin to try to find a bacteriophage system which we might use to solve the genetic code.

Sydney Brenner

I've been to Japan, I've been to China, I've been to Africa, I've been to the Middle East, I've been to Europe a little bit. I've never been to South America.

Colin Quinn

Filmmaking is a great adventure. I'm as excited as a kid to be given tickets to fly suddenly to England, South Africa, America, everywhere. I'm still a 13-year-old kid, flying.

Shekhar Kapur

Slavery in West Africa, and in Rome and in the Mediterranean, was something different than slavery in America.

Edward Ball

The Cold War was waged in a particularly brutal and cynical way in Africa, and Africa seemed powerless to do anything to stop it.

Ryszard Kapuscinski

In Africa, music is for everything, Music was originally used for community. That was what music was for.

Emmanuel Jal

I am climbing Mt. Kilimanjaro in Africa this Summer as a personal physical goal for myself, but also as a way to bring on sponsors and raise awareness and funds to help benefit the programs and initiatives of Chefs for Humanity.

Cat Cora

The uptake on mobile phones in Africa is phenomenal.

Ethan Zuckerman

One of the things that Africa needs, everybody seems to agree, is some measure of debt relief.

Gwen Ifill

One of the biggest things I understood in a program like that was that it allowed more young African American scholars to do field research in the Caribbean and in Africa than had ever happened before in the history of the country and since.

Bernice Johnson Reagon

But now I'm getting that spiritual motivation to visit Africa.

Dennis Brown

I know some of my memories are made up and they are far more powerful than the things that actually happened. For example, I always remember my brother posting me a copy of 'Dubliners' from Africa, but he says he never did.

John Banville

South Africa's increasingly, for example, the largest foreign investor in various other parts of Africa.

Susan Rice

It is important to stress: Africa is also a victim of the September 11 attacks.

Omar Bongo

Well, surely, I am not in charge of South Africa.

Mangosuthu Buthelezi

In most places that are rich in guitar culture, everyone uses their fingers, like in Spain or Africa. In Japan there are string instruments played that way. It is not until you get in the States that you find people using picks.

Kevin Eubanks

Africa is the future.

Youssou N'Dour

Hippos kill more people in Africa annually than any other wild animal.

George Ayittey

Radio is the death and life of Africa.

George Ayittey

The election of Senator Barack Obama brought jubilation across Africa, where millions celebrated him as 'one of their own.'

George Ayittey

Virtually all of Africa's civil wars were started by
politically marginalized or excluded groups.

George Ayittey

What Africa needs to do is to grow, to grow out of debt.

George Ayittey

Miriam Were has made outstanding contributions to public
health in the developing world. She brings basic medical
services to women and children in East Africa.

Liya Kebede

While many applauded Oprah for opening her heart to
young girls in South Africa, some criticized her for not
investing in the youth of America.

Kitty Kelley

I think growing up in South Africa, and then moving to
Canada, I'm just genuinely interested in the difference

between the First World and the Third World, immigration, and how the new, globalized world is beginning to operate. All of those things run through my mind a lot.

Neill Blomkamp

My father was champion of North Africa and he beat the European champ. He was very good, a professional for 12 years. We're from a big family of boxers. My father has seven brothers.

Olivier Martinez

I go back to Africa every year. I have a home there. You know, my grandfather lives back there in Cameroon.

Joakim Noah

My Botswana books are positive, and I've never really sought to deny that. They are positive. They present a very positive picture of the country. And I think that that is perfectly defensible given that there is so much written about Africa which is entirely negative.

Alexander McCall Smith

I have an affinity for Africa, especially East Africa, and Kansas looks very much like that.

Bill Kurtis

Most countries in Africa have the capacity to be great agricultural producers, but they do only subsistence production. So a family will produce for themselves and nothing more. Why? Because of the systems: The markets are not there to go beyond.

Nicolas Berggruen

We cannot do everything in Africa, but doing nothing is not an option.

Lee H. Hamilton

Too often we learn everything about how an African dies, but nothing about how he lives. But they learn and live and love and dream just like we do. That's not to say there are not a hell of a lot of problems in Africa. But there is also another side to that story.

Henning Mankell

My good friend Yao Ming was the first big player in the NBA to come from China. He gave himself to the game and was successful. That inspired the NBA to invest more and do more for the game of basketball. We're building academies not just in China, but in India, Africa, Europe and South America as well.

Dikembe Mutombo

I'm not sure the oil producers are enjoying real growth. That troubles me. For experience has shown that oil can be more of a curse than a blessing. And not only in Africa.

Paul Wolfowitz

The truth is, about the Middle East is, had there been no oil there, it would be like Africa. Nobody is threatening to intervene in Africa.

Wesley Clark

I wasn't born Austrian; I wasn't born German. My roots are from Africa, and I do not have any reason for not wanting to celebrate that. Every time that I can, I like to kind of mention it, you know, just to keep people sort of knowing exactly what's going on. My French is pretty good, but I'm still African, thank you very much.

Jessye Norman

My grandparents all came from Lithuania to South Africa.

Antony Sher

In South Africa, success never presented the problems that it presents in New York. In New York, if you happen to be the flavor of the month, a lot of nonsense comes with it into your life.

Athol Fugard

My mother is a huge fan of my work. I told her about 'Coraline' long before the film was made, and she got the book and read it. She reminded me that when I was about five years old, I used to sit in the kitchen for hours and talk about my 'other' family in Africa, my other mother and father. I had totally forgotten that.

Henry Selick

I've always had a natural affiliation with nature. If I wasn't an actor, I'd be some sort of biologist working in the field in Africa or something.

Callan McAuliffe

I, too, am convinced that our ancestors came from Africa.

Richard Leakey

Africa has been troubled for a long time - well, the world has been troubled ever since I was born.

Hugh Masekela

When I enjoy my surfing, I get good results, and I've always had fun in South Africa.

Joel Parkinson

I really fell in love with Africa.

Jean M. Auel

I would hazard a guess that we have found fossilized human remains of at least a thousand different specimens in South and East Africa, more or less complete at that. I think this is where the prelude to human history was primarily played out.

Richard Leakey

All of the philosophers I studied were white (with a few Eastern exceptions), and, for that matter, they were all male. Africa, the cradle of civilization, seemed to have no footing in the highest form of human thought.

Walter Mosley

I think that black Africa is extremely terrifying. Black Africa can become a maelstrom of warring tribes without the outside world needing to feel the need to do anything about it.

John Keegan

If you come from Africa with your economic poverty and your cultural riches, and you meet someone like Peter Gabriel or a person from a big record company, and they tell you that what you are doing is marvelous, that makes you feel powerful.

Youssou N'Dour

The southward advance of native African farmers with Central African crops halted in Natal, beyond which Central African crops couldn't grow - with enormous consequences for the recent history of South Africa.

Jared Diamond

Zamajobe is great. She's a terrific singer from South Africa.

Lee Ritenour

I work a lot in Africa: Texas and Africa have the best sunsets on the planet, that I've ever seen.

Taylor Kitsch

We emigrated to South Africa and later to Canada so I went to school in several places.

J. Philippe Rushton

There is still a severe and scary amount of extreme poverty in rural parts of India, Pakistan, Afghanistan, Burma and sub-Saharan Africa.

Hans Rosling

I was being groomed as an undergraduate to specialize in Midwestern prehistory, but going back to my teenage days, my interest has always been in our early human ancestors. I wanted to work in Africa.

Donald Johanson

When we look for the origins of all humanity today, let's not just look at Europe, because I think Africa was the cradle, the crucible that created us as Homo sapiens.

Donald Johanson

I think it's a good thing for a president or political leaders to want to put their values or their faith into action. Desmond Tutu did that in South Africa. Martin Luther King Jr. did that here. This is a good thing.

Jim Wallis

Both my parents are English and I was born in West Africa, and I moved around as a kid, lived in Bristol, lived in Buckinghamshire and Surrey as a kid, and then moved when I was 16.

Hugo Weaving

I have always had great respect for former president Mandela. The personal sacrifices he made in order to achieve what was right for the people of South Africa is something I carry with me every day.

Aaron Schock

Big game photography in Africa is mainly done from a vehicle, so then I feel I might as well take the lot.

Nigel Dennis

I'm very aware of what you're talking about as I was involved with the radio in Africa in the same period as I was doing Concrete - I was doing both at the same time.

Pierre Schaeffer

I wanted to wash off the experience of Africa but obviously I couldn't because that's who I was.

Adewale Akinnuoye-Agbaje

Going to Africa was being able to take my volunteering and my passion for hospice one step further.

Torrey DeVitto

People always say 'You do racial comedy.' And I don't, exactly. I do cultural comedy. Because race and culture are two different things. There's black people from America and then there's black people from Africa. Racially, they're the same; culturally, they're extremely different.

Russell Peters

The way people see Africa is mostly dark.

Nneka

I am chairman of the Africa subcommittee in the House of Representatives.

Ed Royce

I had seen AIDS patients in India and Africa, and knowing that people were dying even though drugs existed that could help them was shattering for me.

Yusuf Hamied

There seems to be this sense among even well-meaning Americans that Africa is this black hole of murder and mutilation that can never be fixed, no matter what aid is brought in.

Nicholas D. Kristof

I grew up in Mossel Bay in South Africa on the Garden Route. It's really windy there, and I like it. I enjoy links golf a lot.

Louis Oosthuizen

In my view, the humanity of our world can be measured against the fate of Africa.

Horst Koehler

Whether or not all this came to pass in an East African ditch, I wouldn't like to say. Perhaps it happened in North Africa or further west, but Africa was definitely the place.

Richard Leakey

I've spent quite a bit of time in East Africa.

Greg Wise

Africa's agricultural sector has enormous scope for development, which would benefit both the continent's economy and its people.

Richard Attias

If women are the key to Africa's future - and I believe they are - we must figure out how to take away the barriers to their participation.

Richard Attias

It is my firm belief that action on the issues that matter for Africa must emerge from within Africa itself.

Richard Attias

Africa is a continent that provides so much for the existence of the rest of the world. We go around the world and cultivate so many things.

Djimon Hounsou

Africa is my continent. It is where I opened my eyes.

Djimon Hounsou

Africa touches me. At night, there's this thought in your brain that a million years ago we started here.

Hasso Plattner

I don't want to see that two-tier Senegal, that two-tier Africa, when you have those at the top and those at the bottom, people who are hungry, people who do not have enough to eat.

Youssou N'Dour

I think people should know more of Africa in terms of its joie de vivre, its feeling for life. In spite of the images that one knows about Africa - the economic poverty, the corruption - there's a joy to living and a happiness in community, living together, in community life, which may be missing here in America.

Youssou N'Dour

Music in Africa often contains messages. Music in Senegal, and Africa, is never music for music's sake or solely for entertainment. It's always a vehicle for social connections, discussions and ideas.

Youssou N'Dour

Mugabe's become a disgrace to Africa. And I must say this because I am an African and a lot of us looked up to him back in the 1980s when he was the liberation hero. But he's now turned himself into a murderous despot.

George Ayittey

There's a belief that since Africa got a raw deal from the colonial West, then the Chinese must be Africa's best friend. But the evidence doesn't show that, and the main criticism is that they are building infrastructure in exchange for Africa's resources in deals that are structured to favor China.

George Ayittey

What I find problematic is the suggestion that when, say, Madonna adopts an African child, she is saving Africa. It's not that simple. You have to do more than go there and adopt a child or show us pictures of children with flies in their eyes. That simplifies Africa.

Chimamanda Ngozi Adichie

There are so many things I want to do. Like, I want to get an artist, a musician, a photographer, and a bunch of dancers that I know and just travel across Africa and just film it and just see what happens. Do and learn as much as I possibly can. Luckily, I have a lot more time.

Channing Tatum

My people have a country of their own to go to if they choose... Africa... but, this America belongs to them just as much as it does to any of the white race... in some ways even more so, because they gave the sweat of their brow and their blood in slavery so that many parts of America could become prosperous and recognized in the world.

Josephine Baker

When people talk about South Africa, it's all about lions and elephants. But when we talk about India, we talk about tigers.

Mahendra Singh Dhoni

We will continue to count on your unwavering support and commitment to working with leaders of our continent in bringing about the desired renaissance of Africa.

Thabo Mbeki

The peoples of Asia, Africa, and Latin America have common interest and are in the position to support each other in their anti-imperialist and anti-U.S. struggle. As long as Africa and Latin America are not free.

Kim Il-sung

I am an international leader, the dean of the Arab rulers, the king of kings of Africa and the imam of Muslims, and my international status does not allow me to descend to a lower level.

Muammar al-Gaddafi

Look to Africa, for there a king will be crowned.

Marcus Garvey

When we walk away from global warming, Kyoto, when we are irresponsibly slow in moving toward AIDS in Africa, when we don't advance and live up to our own rhetoric and standards, we set a terrible message of duplicity and hypocrisy.

John F. Kerry

The black man in Africa had mastered the arts and sciences. He knew the course of the stars in the universe before the man up in Europe knew that the earth wasn't flat.

Malcolm X

I have lived in countries that were coming out of conflict: Ireland, South Africa, the Czech republic. People there are overflowing with energy.

Brian Eno

On Saturday, I was a surgeon in South Africa, very little known. On Monday, I was world renowned.

Christiaan Barnard

There is no more apartheid in South Africa than in the United States.

Malcolm X

We of Africa protest that, in this day and age, we should continue to be treated as lesser human beings than other races.

Robert Mugabe

Consumerism diverts us from thinking about women's rights, it stops us from thinking about Iraq, it stops us from thinking about what's going on in Africa - it stops us from thinking in general.

Pink

A squirrel dying in front of your house may be more relevant to your interests right now than people dying in Africa.

Mark Zuckerberg

Africa for the Africans... at home and abroad!

Marcus Garvey

The people made worse off by slavery were those who were enslaved. Their descendants would have been worse off today if born in Africa instead of America. Put differently, the terrible fate of their ancestors benefitted them.

Thomas Sowell

When you see in places like Africa and parts of Asia abject poverty, hungry children and malnutrition around you, and you look at yourself as being people who have well being and comforts, I think it takes a very insensitive, tough person not to feel they need to do something.

Ratan Tata

The people and the cultures of what is known as Africa are older than the word 'Africa.' According to most records, old and new, Africans are the oldest people on the face of the earth. The people now called Africans not only influenced the Greeks and the Romans, they influenced the early world before there was a place called Europe.

John Henrik Clarke

Most of all, I dislike this idea nowadays that if you're a black person in America, then you must be called African-American. Listen, I've visited Africa, and I've got news for everyone: I'm not an African.

Whoopi Goldberg

We have a vision of South Africa in which black and white shall live and work together as equals in conditions of peace and prosperity.

Oliver Tambo

I can't understand why the front pages of newspapers can cover bird flu and swine flu and everybody is up in arms about that and we still haven't really woken up to the fact that so many women in sub-Saharan Africa - 60 percent of people in - infected with HIV are women.

Annie Lennox

South Africa is labouring to find its revolutionary path; the colours of the Rainbow Nation have difficulty blending together; the wealthy elites (white, black or Indian) profit from de facto segregation.

Tariq Ramadan

If there are dreams about a beautiful South Africa, there are also roads that lead to their goal. Two of these roads could be named Goodness and Forgiveness.

Nelson Mandela

Nelson Mandela was an outstanding leader and a mentor for me. I was in South Africa at the time he was released. I was in South Africa when he was inaugurated as the first president.

Gail Kelly

I was the most Australian child ever in the world, even though my home was in Africa.

Mem Fox

I'm doing a lot of things in Africa. I've formed a company with two friends of mine called Made In Africa and we are doing a lot of important things across the continent.

Ozwald Boateng

When I was in South Africa, I went for dinner with some friends, and I knew more about their history than they did - it just hasn't been told.

David Harewood

One of the biggest development issues in the world is the education of girls. In the United States and Europe, it has been accepted, but not in Africa and the developing countries.

Harri Holkeri

There is a movement in club football, which I don't necessarily consider a prime example of solidarity, because it leads us to conclude the rich are getting richer and they are using everything in the market to create an exodus from Africa.

Sepp Blatter

After reading Graham Greene and Joseph Conrad when I was a student at Yale, I wanted to live in the world they captured in their books. I had had some experience living in Africa. I was drawn to that kind of adventure.

Leslie Cockburn

I once knew a girl who didn't know where anywhere was in the world. Not a clue. I asked her if she knew where Africa was and she answered, 'Is it the orange one on a map?'

Matt Roper

Africans are on the front lines of humanitarian efforts, distributing life-saving aid in dangerous environments. Africans comprise the vast majority of peacekeepers in civil conflict on that continent. Africans for the most part lead peace negotiations for the wars being fought in Africa.

John Prendergast

Through my years of working on war and peace in Africa, I have learned that there are solutions to some of the greatest human rights challenges, and we all can be a part of those solutions.

John Prendergast

Al Qaeda attacked the U.S.S. Cole and bombed several U.S. embassies in East Africa in the late 1990s. We knew who did it, but we didn't go after them. Instead, we beefed up security at our embassies and changed the Navy's rules of engagement. It only served to embolden Al Qaeda.

Kathleen Troia McFarland

I skated in ice shows all over Europe and South Africa for 20 years. I love to ice skate.

Kenny Baker

Some countries that are close to Europe that already hold Deutschemarks, clearly would automatically hold euros, those are countries in Eastern Europe mainly, a few countries in Africa.

Robert C. Solomon

The memoirs that have come out of Africa are sometimes startlingly beautiful, often urgent, and essentially life-affirming, but they are all performances of courage and honesty.

Alexandra Fuller

Most of my career has been spent overseas in Africa or in Europe.

Bruce Wilkinson

I was raised in a spirit of the importance of service to your fellow man. My mom is a senator back home in South Africa. My father is a very caring and generous individual.

Adhir Kalyan

It was but then, when you're, one of the great poisonous events that have infected us all who were in South Africa is that the idea of difference is drip fed into your veins. It's that that you fight.

Janet Suzman

In South Africa, being Chinese meant I wasn't white and I wasn't black. I trained in Baragwanath Hospital, the largest black hospital in South Africa. That was around 1976, the time of the Soweto Uprising, when police fired on children and students who were protesting. I was part of the group of interns who volunteered to treat them.

Patrick Soon-Shiong

I was disappointed not to be able to interview Mr. Clinton. I met him two years ago. I was looking forward to talking with him about issues from Africa to terrorism.

Jonathan Dimbleby

I started as an engineer. I migrated to philosophy and international politics. And I did my studies about African - Africa democracy and democratization in Africa, taking Kenya as a model. And then, while I was doing so in 1996 in South Africa, Al Jazeera was established. So they requested me to be an analyst on African affairs.

Wadah Khanfar

The U.K. and the U.S. could not have been built today without Africa's aid. It is all the resources that were taken from Africa, including human, that built these countries today! So when they try to give back, we shouldn't be on the defensive.

Ngozi Okonjo-Iweala

Whenever I have a little time off, I try to go back to my farm in South Africa. I'll spend time with my family and hunt antelope, kudu and springbok. During a 2010 hunting trip, I tore some ligaments in my ankle when I stepped in a hole.

Louis Oosthuizen

The uniqueness of the United States in human history is the United States is the first global power in human history which emerged far away from Africa or Asia, which is the main land of human history.

Ahmet Davutoglu

I was born in France. I grew up in Africa.

Benjamin Millepied

As African economies boom and businesses are created, one of the big questions this growth raises is that of third-level education: how can Africa develop a knowledge infrastructure to rival that of the west, a sort of Harvard University in Africa?

Richard Attias

Bringing more large sporting events to Africa would help the continent develop sports policies and at the same time optimize its peoples' chances of achieving competitive success.

Richard Attias

As a young boy, I had strange dreams of affecting people and somehow being instrumental in changing the makeup of Africa and helping to improve life there.

Djimon Hounsou

One of the things I find extremely challenging about the continent of Africa is that when the immediate needs and the social needs of people are not met, that kills dreams, and it's all about survival.

Djimon Hounsou

When most people in the West think about Africa, is their first thought about the game reserves and who's chasing gazelles, or are they looking at Africans as people who are equally equipped to do great things, as in the West?

Djimon Hounsou

They are responsible for starting this relationship and wanting to help Africa. The United States is very well suited for this as they are a country that has the capacity, they have better access to technology and they are a successful country.

Phumzile Mlambo-Ngcuka

I grew up in a very strong, nuclear family. My father was a sportsman. He represented South Africa in a couple of sports, so he was a very positive person and someone who encouraged you to be your best and give your best with everything that you do.

Gail Kelly

Swaziland is a small part of south-east Africa, the last country in the continent to gain its independence.

Richard Grant

The attacks on the Paris Metro in the 1990s were committed by members of the local Muslim community, immigrants from the Maghreb region of North Africa.

Otto Schily

We will win the battle for Africa, which is in effect a battle for Humanity.

Abdoulaye Wade

It's strange; when I was younger and people would ask, 'Where are you from?', I'd say, 'West Africa', which was odd because I'm obviously not African, but it was my home.

William Boyd

There is a greater fatigue concerning the African problem today than five or 10 years ago. The situation now in Africa is worse today than it was 10 years ago.

Boutros Boutros-Ghali

I usually make sure that my stories are from Africa or my own background so as to highlight the cultural background at the same time as telling the story.

Buchi Emecheta

I have long argued that, if China and the United States were interested in pursuing a strategic partnership, Africa is the best place to start, as neither enters the situation with past colonial baggage, and both possess interests that are quite complementary.

Thomas P.M. Barnett

Living here in North America - I have been Americanized. When I go back home now, there are things that I have far less tolerance for in South Africa. We've come such a long way in terms of race relations and the economy as well as people's willingness to move on. There are still a lot of things that are frustrating about being in South Africa.

Kandyse McClure

I didn't do very well when I was at school, so my dad gave me the opportunity to travel in Africa. I drove from London to Nairobi. It was incredible.

Sean Pertwee

Africa has lost its dream, and when people don't have a dream and don't pursue it, they flounder. People are shocked that I would move to Africa. But I say the place of greatest need is the place of greatest opportunity.

Bruce Wilkinson

Poor laborers from all parts of Asia as well as Africa, the Americas and even Europe are transported by plane each day to wealthier nations where low-tier jobs are plentiful;

sometimes the travelers board without even knowing their final destination.

Alan Huffman

They don't have the news media set up in Africa that we do in the United States, where televisions are so accessible and newspapers and magazines are able to educate people.

Matthew Modine

Africa needs access to markets.

Jakaya Kikwete

One of the things about being raised British in Africa is that you get this double whammy of toughness. The continent in place itself made you quite tough. And then you've got this British mother whose entire being rejects 'coddling' in case it makes you too soft. So there's absolutely nothing standing between you and a fairly rough experience.

Alexandra Fuller

When I went to live in South Africa, I immediately began to understand what went wrong. Because here was a place supposed to be under apartheid - I arrived there in 1991 - but here a black person had more say and had more influence over his white government than an average Kenyan had over the Moi government.

Binyavanga Wainaina

I've wanted to be an actor since I was 6 years old. I was literally picked off the streets of Paris... while I was modeling there. I was asked to audition for Oliver Stone's 'Alexander.' I didn't get the part, but that led to commercials and roles in South Africa.

Tanit Phoenix

If we continue doing the right things in Africa, we can create a very exciting and competitive global market here.

Patrice Motsepe

I helped found Artists for New South Africa, but it used to be called Artists for Free South Africa. Alfre Woodard and a bunch of us started this.

Mary Steenburgen

You can't get a degree at Tisch College. It serves as an amplifier for what your focus is. If you're an engineer, you can take courses on understanding how to move a river in Africa to bring hydroelectric power to a community.

Jonathan Tisch

It turns out that, if you want to know what the U.S. military is doing in Africa, it's advantageous to be connected to a large engineering or construction firm looking for business.

Nick Turse

What the military will say to a reporter and what is said behind closed doors are two very different things - especially when it comes to the U.S. military in Africa.

Nick Turse

While a handful of countries and a small number of people are leading ample life, dozens of countries and billions of people in Africa, Asia and Latin America are being left in absolute poverty.

Tran Duc Luong

I represent my country, but I also represent the continent of Africa when I play in Europe. That's why it's important to try to achieve something big.

Yaya Toure

The mentality with African and European people is different. In Africa, when you come from a difficult life, when it's not so easy to eat, not so easy to survive, you respect money when you start to earn it, and you respect people more. When you respect people, they will respect you, and your life is better for that.

Yaya Toure

In my own creations, the earliest influence came from the ancient civilisations of Egypt, China, Africa and Persia. In fact, one of my earlier creations was a range of tunics, made from silk procured from the islands of Madagascar.

Mary McFadden

I've seen so many screw-ups of representations of South Africa, and it makes me so angry every time.

Lauren Beukes

Only in South Africa could you have a change in government without civil war. If there wasn't the depth of love and caring among our people, this would not have happened.

Patrice Motsepe

Building capacities for the young generation is going to make a better generation and a better future tomorrow for Africa.

Corneille Ewango

I started to work on a feature-length script about pirates in Somalia, but I knew that there was something I was missing, which was that I didn't know what day-to-day life looked like and felt like in East Africa. So I decided I had to go.

Cutter Hodierne

In committing an estimated 3,000 U.S. forces to join international Ebola relief efforts in West Africa, President

Obama seems to be fulfilling the plans of highly influential progressive groups who seek to transform the American military into more of a social-work organization.

Aaron Klein

Most Americans know nothing about the African forest, and it seems to them a very scary, spooky dangerous place. I've spent a lot of time in the forests of central Africa. I know they're beautiful places that contain a lot of different kinds of creatures, including some that carry Ebola.

David Quammen

Now in the 1980s, I happened to notice that if you look at an aerial photograph of an African village, you see fractals. And I thought, 'This is fabulous! I wonder why?' And of course I had to go to Africa and ask folks why.

Ron Eglash

With the discovery of Zinjanthropus at Olduvai Gorge in 1959, my grandmother Mary Leakey pioneered the research in East Africa with my grandfather Louis. Many more spectacular fossil finds have since been made, both in

Africa and elsewhere, by many researchers driven to understand our past.

Louise Leakey

One time I got fan mail that was from Africa. It's really neat.

Scarlett Pomers

I did do an American pilot, but it wasn't shot in America, it was shot in South Africa. It was called 'The Philanthropist,' and it was for NBC.

Dominique McElligott

I would love to produce a film. I have written a script and am in the process of writing another, so maybe it will happen down the road. I would love to do a film in Africa.

Judi Shekoni

Africa is not fulfilling people's hopes and aspirations. African leaders have not had an agenda that included governing Africa so that people would find their careers, their life, dreams and visions fulfilled here.

Ama Ata Aidoo

Acting is rare. You can be rehearsing Ibsen with Sir Richard Eyre and suddenly he has to take a call on his mobile telling him his friend Arthur Miller has died. Or you can come back from a job on the Isle of Man to be told by your agent you're going straight out to South Africa on another shoot. There's not even any time to wash your pants.

Jamie Sives

I moved to New York for love, and it was a disaster, in 2000. And then I had American friends who had lived in South Africa, and they were in Chicago. They said, 'Come and spend some time with us, and we'll help you get over it.'

Lauren Beukes

Congo, my country, has the largest forest in Africa, maybe the second-largest in the world. I was born in a forest area, and when I was growing up, I assisted my uncle, who was a poacher. That was good, because it grew my passion for protecting the forest and plants.

Corneille Ewango

I actually had the good fortune to work with Nick Hoult on 'Mad Max' in Africa, so we became really fast friends.

Josh Helman

I started out doing something little. I went to Africa to spend five weeks putting roofs on a building. I seen the small child that stepped on a land mine. Three months later, I'm back helping pull the land mines out. Little things just kept getting bigger and bigger and bigger.

Sam Childers

Like its agriculture, Africa's markets are highly under-capitalized and inefficient. We know from our work around the continent that transaction costs of reaching the market, and the risks of transacting in rural, agriculture markets, are extremely high. In fact, only one third of agricultural output produced in Africa even reaches the market.

Eleni Zaude Gabre-Madhin

Africa is the second-largest continent, a landmass second from Asia. It also is the second most populated continent, with 900 million people. In fact - coming back to the land mass - Africa is so big that you could fit in the continental United States, China, and the entire Europe into Africa and still have space.

Euvin Naidoo

I grew up in South Africa, but like many people at that time, I couldn't bear living in the country. The main motivation for moving to Britain was to get away.

Manfred Mann

Before I went to jail, I was active in politics as a member of South Africa's leading organization - and I was generally busy from 7 A.M. until midnight. I never had time to sit and think.

Nelson Mandela

Europe became rich because it exploited Africa; and the Africans know that.

Desmond Tutu

In February 2004, the two traditional torturers of Haiti - France and the United States - combined to back a military coup and send President Aristide off to Africa. The U.S. denies him permission to return to the entire region.

Noam Chomsky

The biggest lesson from Africa was that life's joys come mostly from relationships and friendships, not from material things. I saw time and again how much fun Africans had with their families and friends and on the sports fields; they laughed all the time.

Andrew Shue

I'm not talking about Russia in my music. I've never been to Russia. I'm not talking about Africa, Switzerland, China. I'm talking about me being American and growing up in a crazy world and helping to reflect all different sides of life.

Nas

Ridiculous yachts and private planes and big limousines won't make people enjoy life more, and it sends out terrible messages to the people who work for them. It would be so much better if that money was spent in Africa - and it's about getting a balance.

Richard Branson

Africa and its people are the most written about and the least understood of all of the world's people. This condition started in the 15th and the 16th centuries with the beginning of the slave trade system. The Europeans not only colonialized most of the world, they began to colonialize information about the world and its people.

John Henrik Clarke

I love Africa in general South Africa and West Africa, they are both great countries.

Paris Hilton

A genocide in Africa has not received the same attention that genocide in Europe or genocide in Turkey or genocide in other part of the world. There is still this kind of basic discrimination against the African people and the African problems.

Boutros Boutros-Ghali

Rwanda, which is one of the younger independent states in Africa, must be regarded as a model of how great human trauma can be transformed to commence true reconstruction of people. Human trauma can lead to stunted growth and mass withdrawal.

Wole Soyinka

For as long as I can remember, I have been passionately intrigued by 'Africa,' by the word itself, by its flora and fauna, its topographical diversity and grandeur; but above all else, by the sheer variety of the colors of its people, from tan and sepia to jet and ebony.

Henry Louis Gates

It's estimated that across Africa 100 elephants are killed for their tusks every day. It takes nothing more than simple math to get to what that adds up to in a year, and it's a distressing figure.

Graydon Carter

It always struck me that Africa was, in a strange way, a futuristic place and had elements and vibes and spirits that were going to inform the future. Africa Express is an attempt to engage that power outside Africa, and for everyone to benefit from it.

Damon Albarn

I've still not written as well as I want to. I want to write so that the reader in Des Moines, Iowa, in Kowloon, China, in Cape Town, South Africa, can say, 'You know, that's the truth. I wasn't there, and I wasn't a six-foot black girl, but that's the truth.'

Maya Angelou

For Africa to move forward, you've really got to get rid of malaria.

Bill Gates

It's a blessing that South Africa has a man like Nelson Mandela.

Desmond Tutu

Using the power you derive from the discovery of the truth about racism in South Africa, you will help us to remake our part of the world into a corner of the globe on which all - of which all of humanity can be proud.

Oliver Tambo

Everyone is related to Africa; everyone comes from Africa. We are all distant relatives.

Damian Marley

My family has very strong women. My mother never laughed at my dream of Africa, even though everyone else did because we didn't have any money, because Africa was the 'dark continent', and because I was a girl.

Jane Goodall

Everybody now admits that apartheid was wrong, and all I did was tell the people who wanted to know where I come from how we lived in South Africa. I just told the world the truth. And if my truth then becomes political, I can't do anything about that.

Miriam Makeba

Every day I get to 'Think' and work on everything from digitizing electric grids so they can accommodate renewable energy and enable mass adoption of electric cars, helping major cities reduce congestion and pollution, to developing new micro-finance programs that help tiny businesses get started in markets such as Brazil, India, Africa.

Ginni Rometty

Yesterday in this country we had people die of hunger and malnutrition. In some parts of this country, the infant mortality rate rivals that of sub-Saharan Africa. We have a public education system that ranks below that of almost any other Western nation.

Alcee Hastings

What I quickly discovered is that our so-called new South Africa has as much material for a story-teller as the old one. The landscape hasn't really changed. Who is in power now is different to who was in power then, but the squatter camps grow like cancer, the rich get richer, the poor get poorer.

Athol Fugard

Shakespeare is absolutely big in Africa. I guess he's big everywhere. Growing up, Shakespeare was the thing. You'd learn monologues and you'd recite them. And just like hip-hop, it made you feel like you knew how to speak English really well. You had a mastery of the English language to some extent.

Ishmael Beah

One of the most amazing locations I've ever been is the top of the volcano in Tanzania, Africa. It's an actual volcano where you really have this lava every day.

Jan de Bont

Those who invest in South Africa should not think they are doing us a favor; they are here for what they get out of our cheap and abundant labor, and they should know that they are buttressing one of the most vicious systems.

Desmond Tutu

The murder of Lumumba, in which the U.S. was involved, in the Congo destroyed Africa's major hope for development. Congo is now total horror story, for years.

Noam Chomsky

The first light of human consciousness and the world's first civilizations were in Africa.

John Henrik Clarke

Let's face it - think of Africa, and the first images that come to mind are of war, poverty, famine and flies. How many of us really know anything at all about the truly great ancient African civilizations, which in their day, were just as splendid and glorious as any on the face of the earth?

Henry Louis Gates

Having travelled to some 20 African countries, I find myself, like so many other visitors to Africa before me, intoxicated with the continent. And I am not referring to the animals, as much as I have been enthralled by them during safaris in Kenya, Tanzania and Zimbabwe. Rather, I am referring to the African peoples.

Dennis Prager

It is unfortunate that so much of the history of Africa has been written by conquerors, foreigners, missionaries and adventurers. The Egyptians left the best record of their history written by local writers.

John Henrik Clarke

Leaders in Africa are so corrupt that we are certain if we put dogs in uniforms and put guns on their shoulders, we'd be hard put to distinguish them.

Stokely Carmichael

I'd move to Los Angeles if New Zealand and Australia were swallowed up by a tidal wave, if there was a bubonic plague in England and if the continent of Africa disappeared from some Martian attack.

Russell Crowe

I am the hero of Africa.

Idi Amin

Well, Nigeria has played a constructive role in peacekeeping in various parts of West Africa. But unless and until Nigeria itself is democratic and respects human rights, it too may well be a source of much greater instability as political repression limits the ability of the people of Nigeria to achieve their full potential.

Susan Rice

Imagine - four years you could have spent travelling around Europe meeting people, or going to the Far East of Africa or India, meeting people, exchanging ideas, reading all you wanted to anyway, and instead I wasted it at Roosevelt.

Shel Silverstein

Nyasaland was the perfect country for a volunteer. It was friendly and destitute; it was small and out-of-the-way. It had all of Africa's problems - poverty, ignorance, disease.

Paul Theroux

Racial discrimination, South Africa's economic power, its oppression and exploitation of all the black peoples, are part and parcel of the same thing.

Oliver Tambo

I'd like to go on a hardcore safari in Africa, something off the beaten track with anti-poaching people and camping out in the savannah.

Dominic Monaghan

You can say I had a severe case of 'Roots' envy. I wanted to be like Alex Haley, and I wanted to be able to... do my family tree back to the slave ship and then reverse the Middle Passage, as I like to put it, and find the tribe or ethnic group that I was from in Africa.

Henry Louis Gates

Europe and Africa share proximity and history, ideas and ideals, trade and technology. You are tied together by the ebb and flow of people. Migration presents policy challenges - but also represents an opportunity to enhance human development, promote decent work, and strengthen collaboration.

Ban Ki-moon

I can't on my own change the regime in South Africa or teach the Palestinians to learn to live with the Israelies, but I can start with me.

River Phoenix

When people said Africa would change me, I didn't understand what they meant. To see the poverty in the townships, for instance, is overwhelming. I found it heart-wrenching to see young children walking barefoot and hungry in the dirt. I'm the kind of person who wants to change the world right here and now, so I got frustrated.

Jennifer Hudson

Education, particularly higher education, will take Africa into the mainstream of globalization.

John Agyekum Kufuor

People wonder why I love Africa so much. I say this is where I was born and raised. My roots are in Africa; that's were I developed.

Dikembe Mutombo

When the first fossils began to be found in eastern Africa, in the late 1950s, I thought, what a wonderful marriage this was, biology and anthropology. I was around 16 years old when I made this particular choice of academic pursuit.

Donald Johanson

Africa's informal economy is one of the most innovative and inventive environments in the world. Yet it is an environment with little regulation in which workers are often exposed to hard conditions and live without a safety net.

Richard Attias

For Africa to me... is more than a glamorous fact. It is a historical truth. No man can know where he is going unless he knows exactly where he has been and exactly how he arrived at his present place.

Maya Angelou

The titanic effort that has brought liberation to South Africa, and ensured the total liberation of Africa, constitutes an act of redemption for the black people of the world.

Nelson Mandela

I started writing as a child. But I didn't think of myself actually writing until I was in college. And I had gone to Africa as a sophomore or something - no, maybe junior - and wrote a book of poems. And that was my beginning. I published that book.

Alice Walker

Russians not only vehemently despise blacks, they believe Africa begins at the Ukraine border.

P. J. O'Rourke

In the literal sense, there has been no relevant evolution since the trek from Africa. But there has been substantial progress towards higher standards of rights, justice and freedom - along with all too many illustrations of how remote is the goal of a decent society.

Noam Chomsky

Some taxpayers may object to a print journalism bailout on the grounds that it mostly benefits the liberal elite. And we can't blame taxpayers for being reluctant to subsidize the reportorial careers of J-school twerps who should have joined the Peace Corps and gone to Africa to 'speak truth to power' to Robert Mugabe.

P. J. O'Rourke

In 1963, the U.N. Security Council declared a voluntary arms embargo on South Africa. That was extended to a mandatory embargo in 1977. And that was followed by economic sanctions and other measures - sometimes officials, countries, cities, towns - some organized by popular movements.

Noam Chomsky

Niger is not an isolated island of desperation. It lies within a sea of problems across Africa - particularly the 'forgotten emergencies' in poor countries or regions with little strategic or material appeal.

Desmond Tutu

When I walk up on that shore in Florida, I want millions of those AARP sisters and brothers to look at me and say, 'I'm going to go write that novel I thought it was too late to do.

I'm going to go work in Africa on that farm that those people need help at. I'm going to adopt a child. It's not too late, I can still live my dreams.'

Diana Nyad

You see, Africa makes a fool of our idea of justice. It makes a farce of our idea of equality. It mocks our pieties. It doubts our concern. It questions our commitment. Because there is no way we can look at what's happening in Africa, and if we're honest, conclude that it would ever be allowed to happen anywhere else.

Bono

There is always something new out of Africa.

Pliny the Elder

South Africa belongs to all who live in it, black and white.

Thabo Mbeki

When you go to Africa, and you see children, they're usually barefoot, dirty and in rags, and they'd love to go to school.

Annie Lennox

As an adolescent I wrote comic books, because I read lots of them, and fantasy novels set in Malaysia and Central Africa.

Umberto Eco

Every Teen Challenge ministry is responsible for raising its own finances, but we assist these works with finances, prayer and counseling, especially overseas in areas such as Siberia, Africa, South America.

David Wilkerson

Nigeria has had the misfortune - no, the fortune - of seeing the worst face of capitalism anywhere in Africa. The masses have seen it, they are disgusted, and they want an alternative.

Wole Soyinka

Life expectancy in many parts of Africa can be something around the age of thirty five to thirty eight. I mean you're very fortunate if you live to that age. In fact when I went to Uganda for the first time one of the things that occurred to me was that I saw very few elderly people.

Annie Lennox

Africa doesn't leap on you immediately; it seeps slowly, and it's incredibly important to be respectful and humble there.

Jill Scott

Today when we say the West we are already referring to the West and to Russia. We could use the word 'modernity' if we exclude Africa, and the Islamic world, and partially China.

Aleksandr Solzhenitsyn

As a small child in England, I had this dream of going to Africa. We didn't have any money and I was a girl, so everyone except my mother laughed at it. When I left school, there was no money for me to go to university, so I went to secretarial college and got a job.

Jane Goodall

If there was no black man there would be no Rock'n'Roll. The beat, the rhythms of Africa are what created Rock'n'Roll and Jazz.

Ray Manzarek

My thinking was taught to tribes in South Africa like the Zulus and Xhosas. At the time there were about 210 fights breaking out among them every month, but after they listened to my lessons, this fell to just four.

Edward de Bono

Our foreign policy has made a wreck of this planet. I'm always in Africa... And when I go to these places I see American policy written on the walls of oppression everywhere.

Harry Belafonte

Inside me I'm Ghanaian, and I'm proud to be African. But of course I'm Italian. I was born in Italy. I've never been to Africa in my life, but I will go one day.

Mario Balotelli

I had to wear a fat suit to play Mma Ramotswe in 'The No 1 Ladies' Detective Agency.' She's described as being like a small elephant, but she loves her body and size. When we were filming in Africa, it was 110F. It was torturous. I drank a lot of water and ate cucumbers all the time, and underneath the fat suit, I shed pounds - I couldn't help it.

Jill Scott

The African American's relationship to Africa has long been ambivalent, at least since the early nineteenth century, when 3,000 black men crowded into Bishop Richard Allen's African Methodist Episcopal Church in Philadelphia to protest noisily a plan to recolonize free blacks in Africa.

Henry Louis Gates

I'd say the best is when I was in Africa, I saw a hippo in a house. Someone had a pet hippo. And they're meant to be one of the most dangerous animals on the planet, and they had one that was sort of just wandering in and out of their house, just sort of roaming about.

Karl Pilkington

I was there during the first elections in South Africa. I watched them take down the apartheid flag and raise the new flag.

Al Sharpton

Although prefabrication has a long history - the ancient Romans shipped pre-cut stone columns, pediments, and other architectural elements to their colonies in North Africa, where the numbered parts were reassembled into temples - the idea took on a new impetus with the technological advances of the Industrial Revolution.

Martin Filler

I'm the cofounder of Keep a Child Alive. We provide medicine for families affected by HIV and AIDS in places like Africa and India.

Alicia Keys

I received so many hate letters when I breast-fed a starving baby in Africa. I was in Sierra Leone in 2009 and I was weaning my child at that time - she was not there with me. There was a hungry baby who was crying because his mother had no milk, and I thought, 'Why throw away my milk if I can give it to a baby who needs it?'

Salma Hayek

South Africa gives me a perspective of what's real and what's not real. So I go back to South Africa to both lose myself and gain awareness of myself. Every time I go back, it doesn't take long for me to get caught into a very different thing. A very different sense of myself.

Dave Matthews

I chose 'No. 1 Ladies' Detective,' or I'll say it chose me, and it was an absolute blessing, for the experience of being in Africa for seven months and learning so many different things, from languages to foods to greetings. On so many levels, it was an incredible experience.

Jill Scott

I found there's a fairly blatant racism in America that's already there, and I don't think I noticed it when I lived here as a kid. But when I went back to South Africa, and

then it's sort of thrust in your face, and then came back here
- I just see it everywhere.

Dave Matthews

When I was in the Peace Corps I never made a phone call. I
was in Central Africa; I didn't make a phone call for two
years. I was in Uganda for another four years and I didn't
make a phone call. So for six years I didn't make a phone
call, but I wrote letters, I wrote short stories, I wrote books.

Paul Theroux

There are cultural issues everywhere - in Bangladesh, Latin
America, Africa, wherever you go. But somehow when we
talk about cultural differences, we magnify those
differences.

Muhammad Yunus

I was born in Africa. I came to California because it's really
where new technologies can be brought to fruition, and I
don't see a viable competitor.

Elon Musk

Even though I support the blue side of Manchester's football heritage, I don't really mind that wherever I go in the world it's not Manchester City that starts the conversation. 'Ah, yes, Manchester United,' is the response when I say where I come from. It's commonplace everywhere - in Europe, Africa, Asia and even the U.S.

Lucy Powell

White rhythm is waltzes, marches, and the polka. In Africa, rhythm is used for a celebratory groove, but white rhythm doesn't have such an enormous vocabulary of spirits. It's basically militant.

Joni Mitchell

As a citizen of this country, I've got to be honest to the people of South Africa.

Jacob Zuma

People talk about doom-laden scenarios happening in the future: they are happening in Africa now. You can see it perfectly clearly. Periodic famines are due to too many people living on land that can't sustain them.

David Attenborough

Africa has been going through so much for so many years; it's time that it stands up the way other nations are standing up.

Nas

It's not difficult in South Africa for the ordinary person to see the link between capitalism and racist exploitation, and when one sees the link one immediately thinks in terms of a socialist alternative.

Joe Slovo

South Africa was to evolve into the most pernicious example of the criminal practise of colonial and white minority domination.

Thabo Mbeki

I've been to Africa three times. All right? You can't bring Western reasoning into the culture. The same way you can't bring it into fundamental Islam.

Bill O'Reilly

I'm not a prophet; I can only use historical reality to come to a view of the future, and my view is that Africa will return to being African and not European. The advent of colonialism was foreign to the country itself, but it will return to what it was before the Europeans arrived.

Wilbur Smith

When Nelson Mandela walked free, the world sang with joy. Ever since, South Africa has stood as a beacon of hope for Africa.

Ban Ki-moon

I got my love of animals from the Dr. Doolittle books and my love of Africa from the Tarzan novels. I remember my mum taking me to the first Tarzan film, which starred Johnny Weissmuller, and bursting into tears. It wasn't what I had imagined at all.

Jane Goodall

If you followed the media you'd think that everybody in Africa was starving to death, and that's not the case; so it's important to engage with the other Africa.

Chimamanda Ngozi Adichie

I feel as if I go to Africa, I may never come back. I'm just going to live with the animals and adopt an elephant, and it's going to be my friend.

Dianna Agron

Africa is probably one of the most beautiful places I have ever been.

Matthew McConaughey

I am making this trip to Africa because Washington is an international city, just like Tokyo, Nigeria or Israel. As mayor, I am an international symbol. Can you deny that to Africa?

Marion Barry

I cannot be alone in being pretty nauseated by Red Nose Day, or at least its television manifestation. Do I think that wretchedly poor children in Africa should get food and life-saving drugs? Of course. Do I want to be hectored into contributing by celebrities who earn more in a 10-minute slot than many of these families get in a year? Nope.

Simon Hoggart

I haven't traveled in Africa nearly as much as I'd like to. I've been there a few times, and I'd like to learn more about the various cultures in Africa. But that's the basis point of where all of the music that I love is based upon, from Africa to Cuba to Puerto Rico to South America.

Chick Corea

By the time Africa is developed, it will be the wonderland of the world, 'cause it will be able to make use of all the mistakes of other nations. But it nah go just drop out of the sky. So we have to put in work.

Damian Marley

Ethnically, Tuareg describe themselves as white. And they don't look Arab or black. Many Tuareg have light skin, light eyes and sharp angular noses and cheekbones. They are cousins of the Berbers of North Africa. Some legends say the Tuareg are the decedents of an ancient Roman legion that disappeared into the desert two millennia ago.

Richard Engel

My family and our neighbors and friends thought of Africa and its Africans as extensions of the stereotyped characters that we saw in movies and on television in films such as 'Tarzan' and in programs such as 'Ramar of the Jungle' and 'Sheena, Queen of the Jungle.'

Henry Louis Gates

So for everybody who allows themselves to be separated from me because I said 'African' instead of 'Nubian' or 'Black' or 'Kemet' or 'original' or 'Israelite,' don't be so foolish. I say 'African' because the continent of Africa is the land from which we all originate. It is the word that we are most familiar with right now.

Sister Souljah

Being from Africa is the best thing that could have ever, ever happened to me. I cannot see it any other way. All of my fundamental principles that were instilled in me in my home, from my childhood, are still with me.

Hakeem Olajuwon

What I generally get from being in Africa is a sense of warmth and openness. As a stranger, you are always welcomed into people's homes and people are always offering you food. That generosity is incredibly touching.

Naomie Harris

Sometimes I say to myself, what are you doing in this absurd job? Why don't you go to Africa and help people? But I cannot help people, because I am a hypochondriac.

Javier Bardem

Could I say that the reason that I am here today, you know, from the mouth of the State Department itself, is: I should not be allowed to travel because I have struggled for years for the independence of the colonial peoples of Africa.

Paul Robeson

South Africa never leaves one indifferent. Its history, its population, its landscapes and cultures - all speak to the visitor, to the student, to the friend of Africa.

Tariq Ramadan

Working with kids in Soweto in South Africa, it's rough out there. But the bottom line is you've got to go to know. In Cambodia, there are 10,000 landmines. Same in Afghanistan, same in Colombia. I'm totally addicted to traveling.

Quincy Jones

I've got fans and letters from Israel, France Germany, Sweden, London, Africa. They all saying pretty much the same thing, 'Yo, we love you, we need you, put some more music out, please!'

DMX

Despite the hundreds of non-governmental organizations and the continued outpouring of foreign aid, East Africa remains as a region overwhelmed by extreme poverty.

Jacqueline Novogratz

Usually halfway through a book I have a serious depression, so I go on safari on my ranch in South Africa, or fishing off my island in the Seychelles. When I come back and re-read it, I think: 'What was all that about, Smith? It's fine, just get on with it.'

Wilbur Smith

I did go on safari in Kenya when I was 17, with my mother, stepfather and little brother, and I kept a careful journal of the experience that was very helpful in terms of my sensory impressions of Africa. I have traveled quite a bit at distinct times in my life, though now that I have kids I've settled down.

Jennifer Egan

Women in America will have to find an answer for the pressures of work and family, but if you really care about women's issues you have to think about women in the world, especially Africa, Asia and the Middle East.

Gail Collins

God bless Africa, Guard her people, Guide her leaders, And give her peace.

Trevor Huddleston

When I look at the system here and look at my position - not just as a basketball player, but when I look around me at the values of the people and the culture and compare them with the values of where I came from - I feel so blessed to be from Africa.

Hakeem Olajuwon

All of Africa's resources should be declared resources of the state and managed by the nation. Our experience in Bolivia shows that when you take control of natural resources for the people of the town and village, major world change is possible.

Evo Morales

There was really no friendship in modeling, though a certain amount of warmth comes from running into models you know on shoots, because you end up in so many unfamiliar places, from Alaska to Africa.

Carol Alt

What I remember the most really was just running wild there. Barefooted, swimming in dirty lakes, selling fruit, picking mango trees, hoping not to get caught because they don't take kindly to thieves in Africa.

Akon

Americans think African writers will write about the exotic, about wildlife, poverty, maybe AIDS. They come to Africa and African books with certain expectations.

Chimamanda Ngozi Adichie

Africa is poor because its investors and its creditors are unspeakably rich.

Naomi Klein

I think we have got the wood on South Africa, but that does not mean they are not a good team. They intimidate a lot of teams but we intimidate them. There is no disrespect for South Africa; they are a very good team.

Shane Warne

Christianity is the fastest-growing religion in the world; Islam is the second. It's spreading in Asia, Africa, and South America. So the world is in a kind of religious revival, and the atheists are totally flummoxed. They thought they were winning, and now they see that they aren't.

Dinesh D'Souza

For most of my writing life, I've refused to allow myself to believe that writing was a significant form of action. I always felt very uneasy about the fact that all I did was write in a situation as desperate as apartheid South Africa. Whether I was correct or not is a different issue.

Athol Fugard

My heart is in South Africa, through my mum. My mum being from here, me spending a lot of time here as well, I feel most connected to this part of the world.

Roger Federer

Rural communities in Africa, South Asia and Latin America are where the majority of hungry people are and the inequality that exists between women and men in these communities is holding back progress.

Dionne Warwick

I think we have a good team, but soccer fans will know that we're in a really tough group. The three teams in our group are really strong. The Czech Republic is a very good team, Italy is traditionally a powerhouse, and Ghana is one of the best teams in Africa.

Claudio Reyna

Happily, there's a reversal of the brain drain occurring in Ghana now. We're seeing a lot of - actually in Africa - we're seeing a lot of African professionals, you know, returning to the continent to contribute their quota.

John Dramani Mahama

Even though it is the case that poverty is linked to AIDS, in the sense that Africa is poor and they have a lot of AIDS, it's not necessarily the case that improving poverty - at least in the short run, that improving exports and improving development - it's not necessarily the case that that's going to lead to a decline in HIV prevalence.

Emily Oster

If you go to Africa and you're white, you're probably not going to get that much work either. But the fact is that there is a longer history of black integration in the U.S. I don't have any resentment about this: I did the maths, calculated it against my ambition and decided to leave England.

Idris Elba

In Botswana in the Kalahari Desert there's a tented camp called Jack's Camp, which is like old Africa meets Ralph Lauren. The Oriental rugs, the old leather chairs - you feel like you've just jumped out of a Ralph Lauren ad.

Mark Burnett

For you in the West to hear the phrase 'All men are created equal' is to draw a yawn. For us, it's a miracle. We're starting out at rock bottom, man. But South Africa does have soul.

Athol Fugard

I was fortunate enough to visit a lot of beautiful places around the world. The most astonishing and memorable experiences were my trips to Africa and Australia.

Karolina Kurkova

The desert loves me. I love the desert. It's nice to be in the heat in Africa. I love it.

Liya Kebede

The richest persons in Africa are heads of state, governors and ministers. So every 'educated' African who wants to be rich - and there is nothing wrong with wanting to be rich - heads straight into government or politics.

George Ayittey

Actually, today I had to defend the Bush Administration in France again. They refuse to accept, because of their political ideology, that he has actually done more than any American President for Africa. But it's empirically so.

Bob Geldof

I have come to one conclusion: All that I am, all that I aspire to be, all that I was before, is by the grace of God. There are so many women in Africa, and outside Africa, who are more intelligent than I am.

Leymah Gbowee

There's a huge AIDS epidemic in Africa, and one of Bad Boy's plans this year is to give more awareness to that. We're gonna be doing a big charity concert helping to save some of the brothers and sisters in Africa.

Sean Combs

I love going to Africa and stuff. I love going anywhere, really, but I've been to Africa a bunch of times and it's just a beautiful place that needs help, obviously, but helping people that are really thankful is really easy to do. And the people out there always seem so thankful.

Kris Allen

I don't mind snakes. Growing up in South Africa there were a couple a snakes around... and I'm not talking just about the government!

Trevor Rabin

Ultimately the white man should leave the United States and the black people should go back to Africa.

Bobby Fischer

Well, I think by any expectation South Africa has come a tremendously long way. We've seen a society that many people thought couldn't withstand a peaceful transition to democracy without a great deal of violence, in fact, make that transition and do it in relative peace and security.

Susan Rice

Because pandemics almost always begin with the transmission of an animal microbe to a human, it's work that takes me all around the globe - from rain forest hunting camps of central Africa to wild animal markets of east Asia.

Nathan Wolfe

Obama remains frozen in his father's time machine. His anti-colonialism is the anti-colonialism of Africa in the 1950s: state confiscation of land, confiscatory taxation, and so on. My anti-colonialism is the anti-colonialism of India in the 21st century.

Dinesh D'Souza

I grew up in a dictatorship in East Africa.

Teresa Heinz

You know, we're missing so much as African-Americans and we should be concerned about what's going on in Africa.

Chris Tucker

Nigeria is the most populous country in Africa. If Nigeria succeeds at democratic governance it will be an anchor for all of West Africa. Africa needs a strong Nigeria.

Ed Royce

It's not just Ethiopia, but Africa in general - most of the media concentrates on what's not going well. But there is so much beauty there. When you go, it changes everything. It changes you, your life, and the way you see things. The challenge is changing the image of Africa that's been anchored in people for years now.

Liya Kebede